Norvegian "Citron" Chicken
(page 29)

*Poultry
and
Sauces*

Madame Benoit

Encyclopedia of microwave cooking

Poultry and Sauces

Héritage plus

Canadian Cataloguing in Publication Data

Benoit, Jehane, 1904-
  Poultry and sauces

(Encyclopedia of microwave cooking ; 4)
(Héritage+plus)
Issued also in French under title: Les volailles
  et leurs sauces.
Includes index.
ISBN 2-7625-5809-3

1. Microwave cookery. 2. Cookery (Poultry).
3. Sauces. I. Title. II. Series.

TX832.B4813 1985   641.5'882   C86-001252-2

Front cover design: Bouvry Designer Inc.
Front cover and inside photography: Paul Casavant
Conception and research: Marie-Christine Payette
Dishes loaned by courtesy of: Le Curio, Montenach Mall, Beloeil.

Legal Deposit: 4th quarter 1985
Bibliothèque nationale du Québec
National Library of Canada

ISBN: 2-7625-5809-3   Printed in Canada

LES ÉDITIONS HÉRITAGE INC.
300, Arran, Saint-Lambert, Quebec J4R 1K5
(514) 672-6710

Table of Contents

Foreword

The Microwave represents today's ultimate in modern cooking. It is a natural successor to convenience frozen foods, automatic coffee makers, food processors, and so many other electrical appliances which have become timesavers for the whole family, providing more opportunity for other activities.

Another factor, the traditional three meals a day that so often turn into five or even ten meals a day, given today's staggered hours of work, sports, studies. . . for young and old alike. . . means the use of the Microwave as a welcome solution to harried schedules. And, of course, there's the well-known ease with which the Microwave can be moved from kitchen to living room or to the outside barbecue or country cottage. Just plug it in. . . "et voilà". It's ready to operate. While saving on electricity too !

If there were a Microwave theme song, it would have to be: "Getting to know you is getting to love you". So now, here are poultry and game, at their very best when cooked in a Microwave.

Introduction

In the course of time, many changes and modifications have taken place with regard to the preparation and cooking of food, table setting, and the time spent at such tasks. What a journey, going back to the time of the wood stove, which was still part of our daily life, even up to the years 1915 and 1920. Then, suddenly, important changes took place, gas and electricity for cooking, bringing about new kitchen equipment, new methods, savings in time, cleaning made easier, and not the least. . . white and elegant new stoves.

And now! A further gigantic step, which is changing and will continue to change many things... microwave ovens!

You buy a microwave oven, put it in the car, bring it home, place it on the kitchen counter, plug it in, and it's ready for use! And it's so easy for everyone to cook their favorite dishes in a microwave oven.

I, myself, started with the wood stove, and the memory still lingers on of those large slices of homemade bread toasted on top of the stove, and savored with fresh churned butter, homemade jam and café au lait with whole milk. What a delight! Of course, at that time, there was someone to rise at 5 a.m. to light the stove, and in the evening to rake over the ashes. There was a cook to churn the milk and make butter, and who spent innumerable summer hours making all that delicious jam.

Then followed the advent of the gas stove, with its coin-operated meter. If you forgot to feed in those 25¢ pieces, the gas was turned off! Still, it was an improvement over the wood stove. And one day the electric stove made an appearance. . . a miracle! We had seen nothing yet!

Modern technology has brought comfort, ease of work, perfection in cooking, the possibility of retaining the full flavor of food, the incredible reduction in hours of work, and the feasibility for each member of the family to cook his or her own meal, which gives the working mother a freedom she had never known before. This has been my experience: I cook more than ever before, yet my time spent in the kitchen has been reduced considerably. After thirteen years of cooking with microwave ovens, now I couldn't live without one. I have come to realize that you cannot know the true flavor of a vegetable or fish until you cook it in a microwave oven. And I can assure you that you need not learn a whole new cooking method, but simply learn to adapt your cooking to the microwave oven.

Many people have said to me: "I would not have the patience to change all my recipes", and so, I have decided to write this Encyclopedia of Microwave Cooking, so that you may realize how easy this method is once understood.

Microwave cooking is equally convenient for the small family with everyone working outside, as it is for the large family where larger servings are needed. All that's needed is knowing how to proceed.

The importance of knowing your oven

There are many models of microwave ovens, even of the same brand. It is therefore of utmost importance to become well acquainted with your oven, and to know and understand all its features.

What to do

- Once the oven is plugged in, place a bowl of water in it, close the door, and read the operation manual following every step as suggested.
  Example: Heat oven at HIGH for 2 minutes.

Look for Power Select HIGH and program, then look for the START setting; touch to put the oven on. You will then understand how this operation works.

Repeat this procedure for all types of operations, and very soon you will realize how easy it is, and you will understand how your own oven works.

Be Knowledgeable About Microwave Terms

There are many brands of microwave ovens on the market. That is why it is important to understand the language. Read and learn the following notes and microwave cooking will become clear and easy.

High or Full Power

This means a continuous cycle with maximum (100%) output, whatever your brand of oven.
The recipes in each volume of this encyclopedia were prepared for microwave ovens with wattage in the 650 - 700 range. If your oven has a lower output, increase the cooking time slightly according to the conversion chart.

All recipes in this book have been tested in a 650 and a 700-Watt microwave oven.
However, if you are using an oven with less wattage here is a comparative chart which will permit you to adjust the cooking time.

650-700W	500-600W	400-500W
15 seconds	18 seconds	21 seconds
30 seconds	36 seconds	42 seconds
45 seconds	54 seconds	1 minute
1 minute	1 min. 10 sec.	1 min. 25 sec.
2 minutes	2 min. 30 sec.	2 min. 45 sec.
3 minutes	3 min. 30 sec.	4 minutes
4 minutes	4 min. 45 sec.	5 min. 30 sec.
5 minutes	6 minutes	7 minutes
6 minutes	7 min. 15 sec.	8 min. 25 sec.
7 minutes	8 min. 25 sec.	9 min. 45 sec.
8 minutes	9 min. 30 sec.	11 minutes
9 minutes	10 min. 45 sec.	12 min. 30 sec.
10 minutes	12 minutes	14 minutes
15 minutes	18 minutes	20 minutes
20 minutes	24 minutes	27 minutes
25 minutes	30 minutes	34 minutes
30 minutes	36 minutes	41 minutes

This chart gives you an idea of the time needed for any food you cook in an oven with the above wattage.
However, it is always wise, regardless of wattage, to check the cooking when 2 minutes of the cooking period still remain. That's assuming, of course, that the cooking time indicated is over 2 minutes.

Let Stand

Many recipes read "Let stand x minutes after cooking". Since the microwave process of cooking is actually intense molecular vibration, food continues to cook even after the microwave energy is turned off. In a way, the same happens when food is cooked in x time in an ordinary oven and we let it stand.
With microwaves the standing time lets the molecules come to rest. This is just like a bouncing ball that dribbles down to a gradual stopping point. It is often referred to as "aftercook".
When a recipe says "Let stand x minutes, stir and serve," that is exactly what is meant.

Rotate

If your oven has a turntable or a special system, such as Rotaflow, or the microwave oven over the stove which has a hidden turntable that does the same work as the rotating type, then you do not have to rotate the dish in which the food is cooking. Otherwise, give a quarter turn to the dish once or twice during the cooking period.

Microwave-proof Dishes or Utensils

All dishes and utensils suitable for microwave cooking (e.g.: Pyrex, Corning, Micro-Dur, Earthenware casseroles, etc.).

Elevate

This term is most often used for meats. It means placing the roast or chicken, etc., on a rack or an inverted saucer to allow cooking juices to drain off from under the meat.
After microwaving a roast, allow meat to cool slightly, still on a rack to allow surface air to cool it evenly.
Another example: when making muffins or cupcakes, cool for at least 10 minutes, on a rack, to allow air to cool the food evenly.

Variable Power

This describes the choice of power levels that allow you to prepare food in the microwave which normally would be over sensitive to continuous microwave activity. To easily understand this process, it is actually an "on and off" cycle timed for varying amounts of microwave energy, which means that this pulsating action effectively creates slower cooking activity, without your having to worry about it. If your recipe calls for 1/2 power, this equals MEDIUM-SLOW, which is like constant simmering.
When microwave cooking first began, ovens had only "Cook" and "Defrost" cycles. Some of you may still have these ovens, so remember that you effectively "simmer" on the Defrost cycle or whenever 1/2 power or MEDIUM is called for. For all other cooking, use the Cook cycle and add a few minutes to the cooking period called for in the recipe.

Temperature Probe

A thermometer-like, heat sensing device to measure internal temperature of food during microwaving. Use only the "Probe" designed for your oven. It is perfect to cook a roast, by inserting the "Probe" in the meat, connecting it to the oven, then choosing the number referring to the cooking you wish to have; (e.g.: for a rare or well done roast, cook at the line printed on the oven time board and touch number indicated, then oven will start the cooking and at one point will give the degree of temperature needed to have the meat cooked according to your taste). You never have to worry how long it should take, since your oven will do it for you, and to perfection. Prepare the roast according to the recipe you are following.

Note : Never use a conventional thermometer in the microwave oven. There are many other ways to cook in the microwave, so **always be ready to give serious** attention to your oven manual, **and you will soon find** it is all very easy.

13

Degree of Moisture in Food

(1) The degree of moisture in food:
   the higher it is: faster and shorter cooking period. — e.g.: spinach;
   the lower it is: slower and longer cooking period. — é.g.: carrots.
(2) The quantity of liquid added to the food:
   the greater the quantity, the longer the cooking period will be.
(3) The density of produce:
   Porous = faster cooking: tomatoes, spinach, mushrooms, etc.
   More dense = longer cooking: peas, lentils, etc.
(4) Room temperature is the ideal temperature to start cooking:
   Warmer temperature = faster cooking with food at room temperature;
   Colder temperature = longer cooking with food taken from refrigerator or after thawing.
(5) The structure of the food:
   Smaller pieces = faster cooking: a small potato;
   Larger pieces = slower cooking: a large potato.
(6) Often foods are covered during the cooking period to prevent the natural moisture from evaporating because the water in these foods has been activated.
(7) The degree of sugar content determines the degree of heat produced:
   The more sugar, the more intense the heat and the shorter the cooking period: syrup, caramel, etc.
(8) The more fat in food, the faster it will cook.
(9) The arrangement of the food plays an important role:
   4 to 5 potatoes placed in a circle will cook faster than if they were simply placed in the oven.

(10) Degree of moisture - adding of water - density - thickness - structure - covers - amount of sugar - degree of fat - arrangement of food - appropriate accessories - are all key words relating your cooking to the factors of heat, weight and temperature.

How to cook food in the Microwave Oven

Microwaves are a form of high frequency radio wave similar to those used by a radio including AM, FM, and CB.
Electricity is converted into microwave energy by the magnetron tube, and microwaves are approximately four to six inches (10 to 15 cm) long with a diameter of about one-fourth inch (6mm). From the magnetron tube, microwave energy is transmitted to the oven cavity where it is: reflected, transmitted and absorbed.

Reflection

Microwaves are reflected by metal just as a ball is bounced off a wall. That is why the inside of the oven is metal covered with epoxy. A combination of stationary (interior walls) and rotating metal (turntable or stirrer fan) helps assure that the microwaves are well distributed within the oven cavity to produce even cooking.

Transmission

Microwaves pass through some materials such as paper, glass and plastic much like sunlight shining through a window. Because these substances do not absorb or reflect the microwave energy, they are ideal materials for microwave oven cooking containers.

Absorption

During heating, microwaves will be absorbed by food. They penetrate to a depth of about 3/4 to 1½ inches (2 to 4 cm). Microwave energy excites the molecules in the food (especially water, fat and sugar molecules), and causes them to vibrate at a rate of 2,450,000,000 times per second. This vibration causes friction, and heat is produced. If you vigorously rub your hands together, you will feel heat produced by friction. The internal cooking is then done by conduction. **The heat** which is produced by friction is conducted to the center of the food.

Foods also continue to cook by conduction during standing time, which keeps the cooked food warm for 4 to 10 minutes after cooking, and makes it possible to cook 3 to 4 dishes with only one oven, and to serve everything warm.

Example: If your menu calls for a roast, potatoes and green peas, cook the roast first. During its waiting period, cook the potatoes, they will remain warm from 20 to 30 minutes covered with a cloth, then the vegetable with the shortest cooking period.

The dessert may be cooked before the meat, or if it is to be served hot, cook it during the meal and let it stand in the oven. The oven goes off when the bell rings, and the food may be left inside until it is time to serve it.

Cooking equipment

Microwave cooking opens new possibilities in convenience and flexibility for cooking containers. There are new microwave accessories constantly being introduced, but do not feel you need to purchase all new equipment. You will be surprised at the numerous items you already have in your kitchen that are suitable for microwave cooking.

Glass, Ceramic and China

Most of these utensils are excellent for use in the microwave oven. Many manufacturers now identify microwave oven safe dishes. Heat resistant glassware, unless it has metallic trim or decoration, can most always be used. However, be careful about using delicate glassware since it may crack, not from microwave energy, but from the heat of the food.

Here are a few heat-resistant glass cookware items I find invaluable in microwave cookery. You probably have many of these items on your shelf already:
- glass measuring cups
- custard cups
- mixing bowls
- loaf dish
- covered casserole dishes
- oblong baking dish, non-metallic
- cake dishes, round or square, glass
- pie plate, plastic, glass or ceramic
- large bowls, 8 to 10 cups (2 to 2.5 L), with covers
- cake dishes, round, long, square, Pyrex, plastic, "Micro-Dur".

Browning Dish (Corning)

There are two sizes: 8 x 8 x 2 inches (21 x 21 x 5 cm) — 6 cups (1.5 L)
9.5 x 9.5 x 2 inches (24 x 24 x 5 cm) — 10 cups (2.5 L)

There is also a Browning Grill: 8 x 8 inches (21 x 21 cm).

A Browning Dish has a special dielectric coating on the underside. The coating is activated by preheating (uncovered) the empty Browning Dish for no more than 7 minutes for the smaller one or 9 minutes for the larger one or for the grill in the Microwave.

Do not remove dish from oven after preheating, simply place in the preheated dish the steak, or whatever you wish to brown, pressing down on the food with a fork to obtain perfect contact with the bottom of the dish. If the recipe calls for oil or butter or other fat, it must be added after preheating the dish. Brown 5 to 7 minutes or according to recipe. You will be surprised how well browned the food will be. Turn it and let stand in the dish in the Microwave the time it took to brown the bottom part, without heat, as giving it more cooking time will only dry the food. It is then ready to serve.

A Browning Dish can be an extremely handy accessory with many uses: to brown steaks and chops, etc., stir-fry vegetables, cook omelets, reheat pizzas, grill sandwiches, and much more.

Do not limit these items to being browners only! They are just as useful as regular microwave cookware. Without preheating, the base will not get hot so can be used for microwaving vegetables, casseroles, desserts, fish, etc. The Browning Dish cover is used more frequently for this type of cooking.

Browning Dishes are for use in Microwaves only, and not in regular ovens (coating could be scratched by oven racks), or on range top as possible damage to special coating could result.

Do not use Probe with the Browning Dish.

Cooking bags
Cooking bags designed to withstand boiling, freezing or conventional heating are safe to use in the microwave oven. Make six small slits in the top of the bag to allow steam to escape. If you use twist-ties to close the bag, make sure the ends are completely rolled around the bag, not loose, as they could act as an antenna and cause arcing (blue sparks). It is better to use a piece of cotton string or a nylon tie, or a strip cut from the open end of the bag. DO NOT COOK FOOD IN BROWN OR WHITE PAPER BAGS.

Plastic wrap
Plastic wrap such as Saran Wrap™ and others can be used to cover dishes in most recipes. Over an extended heating time, some disfiguration of the wrap may occur. When using plastic wrap as a casserole dish cover, fold back a small section of plastic wrap from the edge of the dish to allow some steam to escape. When removing plastic wrap "covers", as well as any glass lid, be careful to remove it away from you to avoid steam burns. After heating, loosen plastic but let dish stand covered. Please note that it is not always necessary to cover all foods.

Food Covering for Sensor Cooking
When cooking by Sensor method an inch (2.5 cm) of water is needed in the bottom of the dish and the dish must be covered with plastic wrap. The Microwave-safe plastic dish "MICRO-DUR" does not need the plastic wrap as its cover keeps the steam inside the dish.

Aluminum foil
Aluminum foil can be used safely when certain guidelines are followed. Because it reflects microwave energy, foil can be used to advantage in some cases. Small pieces of foil are used to cover areas such as the tips of chicken wings, chicken legs, or roasts that cook more quickly than the rest. Foil is used in these cases to slow or stop the cooking process and prevent overcooking. The strips of foil placed on the edges of a roast or the ends of chicken legs can be removed halfway through the cooking period.

Food characteristics
Food characteristics which affect conventional cooking are more pronounced with microwave heating.

Size and quantity
Microwave cooking is faster than cooking with gas or electricity, therefore the size and quantity of food play an important role in cooking time.

Shape
Uniform sizes heat more evenly. To compensate for irregular shapes, place thin pieces toward the center of the dish and thicker pieces toward the edge of the dish.

Bone and fat
Both affect heating. Bones conduct heat and cause the meat next to it to be heated more quickly*. Large amounts of fat absorb microwave energy and meat next to these areas may overcook.

*See Aluminum foil paragraph.

Starting temperature
Room temperature foods take less time to heat than refrigerator or frozen foods.

Spacing
Individual foods, such as baked potatoes and hors d'oeuvres, will heat more evenly if placed in the oven equal distances apart. When possible, arrange foods in a circular pattern.
Similarly, when placing foods in a baking dish, arrange around the outside of dish, not lined up next to each other. Foods should NOT be stacked on top of each other.

Chicken Breasts Milano
(page 37)

Stirring
Stirring is often necessary during microwave cooking. Recipes advise as to frequency of stirring.

Example: Always bring the cooked outside edges toward the center and the less cooked center portions toward the outside. Some foods should be turned in the container during heating.

Standing time
Most foods will continue to cook by conduction after the microwave oven is turned off. In meat cookery, the internal temperature will rise 5°F to 15°F if allowed to stand, covered, for 10 to 20 minutes. Casseroles and vegetables need a shorter amount of standing time, but this standing time is necessary to allow foods to complete cooking in the center without overcooking on the edges.

Power Select Settings
Some microwave ovens are equipped with multiple Power Select settings: HIGH, MEDIUM-HIGH, MEDIUM, MEDIUM-LOW, DEFROST, LOW, WARM, and DELAY/STAND.
While most foods can be heated on HIGH (full power), certain types of foods, milk for example, will benefit from heating with a reduced amount of energy over a slightly longer time.
This variety of settings offers you complete flexibility in microwave cooking.

IMPORTANT

The following recipes were tested in 650 - 700 watt microwave ovens.

Lower-wattage ovens may necessitate some adjustment in timing. (See chart on page 12).

The recipes in general will serve 6 medium portions or 4 large portions.

17

Power Level Chart

Power	Output	Use
HIGH	100%.................... (700 watts)	Boil water Brown ground meat Cook fresh fruits and vegetables Cook fish Cook poultry (up to 3 lb [1.5 kg]) Heat beverages (not containing milk) Make candy Preheat Browning Dish (accessory)
MEDIUM-HIGH	90%.................... (650 watts)	Heat frozen foods (not containing eggs or cheese) Heat canned foods Reheat leftovers Warm baby food
MEDIUM	70%.................... (490 watts)	Bake cakes Cook meats Cook shellfish Prepare eggs and delicate food
MEDIUM-LOW	50%.................... (360 watts)	Bake muffins Cook custards Melt butter and chocolate Prepare rice
LOW	27%.................... (200 watts)	Less tender cuts of meat Simmer stews and soups Soften butter and cheese
WARM	10%.................... (70 watts)	Keep foods at serving temperature Rise yeast breads Soften ice cream
"Defrost"	35%.................... (245 watts)	All thawing, see Defrosting Charts
"Delay Stand"	0%.................... (0 watts)	Start heating at later time Program stand time after cooking

IMPI — International Microwave Power Institute — is an international institution governing microwave data throughout the world for kitchens, hospitals, etc.
IMPI have set the standards which have been adopted with regard to the designation of Power Settings for Microwave Ovens: HIGH, MEDIUM-HIGH, MEDIUM, MEDIUM-LOW, LOW, REHEAT, DEFROST, START, which must be observed everywhere in the world.

The Turntable

It is to our advantage to study and make use of the innovative technologies in microwave ovens, as they always make it easier for us. Do make sure to read the instructions in your oven manual to learn about and understand the various cooking methods your oven has to offer and their use.
The following are some features which you need to acquaint yourself with in order to take full advantage of them.

Magnetic Turntable

Some ovens are equipped with an automatic magnetic turntable or a small fan in the top of the oven, or an invisible rotating system (whichever is featured in your Microwave, it will be explained in your instruction manual), then you do not have to rotate the dish.
If your Microwave has neither turntable, nor fan, nor invisible rotating system, then you will have to rotate the dish for even cooking as the Microwave may tend to focus more on a definite spot in the food, especially if there is fat in the meat, and remember that they are not always visible. What happens is that the fat parts cook more quickly because the reflection area is not altered, so, of course the cooking dish may be rotated.

Auto Sensor Cooking

The Auto Sensor is yet another wonder of Microwave cooking! The Microwave oven determines the cooking time. You wish to cook either a vegetable, meat, poultry, stew, etc., and are wondering what cooking time to allow. Relax.
If your Microwave features Auto Sensor Cooking it will be indicated on the oven panel with a COOK or INSTA-MATIC, etc. section, and your oven manual will give you instructions as to its use.
Numbers 1 to 7 or 8 are also shown on the panel, each one indicating the type of food for cooking, e.g. A7 Soft Vegetables (brussels sprouts, zucchini, etc.); A8 Hard Vegetables (carrots, etc.) Always refer to your oven manual for precise instructions.
There are two important points to remember when cooking by Auto Sensor (COOK). Whatever the food, a little water must always be added, from 1/4 to 1/3 cup (60 - 80 mL), depending on the quantity, and the dish must be well covered with either plastic wrap or a tight-fitting lid that will hold securely in place throughout the cooking period. There are some dishes, of various shapes and sizes, with a perfect lid for Auto Sensor Cooking which are available on the market. They are called "Micro-Dur".
- It is important that the oven door not be opened during the cooking period. The operation takes place in two stages.
- The selected number appears and remains in the display window until such time as the steam is detected by the humidity sensor, which is inside the oven. At this time a BEEP is heard and the cooking time appears in the display window.

A few hints for reheating food in the Microwave Oven

Like defrosting, reheating a wide variety of foods is a highly appreciated use of a microwave oven. It not only saves time, money and clean-up, but most foods reheat so well that there is little loss of taste. Leftovers take on that "just cooked" flavor which has never been possible when reheating by conventional methods. Many foods are actually better when reheated because they have had time to allow the flavors to blend.
Such foods as spaghetti sauce, lasagna, mashed potatoes, creams, stews are examples of foods whose flavor improves with reheating.

A plate of food

Arrange foods on a microwave-safe plate with thicker or denser portions towards the rim of the plate. Add gravy or butter where desired. Cover plate with waxed paper, reheat at MEDIUM-HIGH for 2 to 3 minutes, checking after 2 minutes.

To reheat by Sensor
Prepare plate in the same manner, cover completely with plastic wrap, and touch pad 1 of Sensor or any other as instructed in your microwave manual, that is, of course, if you have a Sensor pad on your oven. The oven does the work. You do not have to determine the time.

Casseroles
Stir well and add a small amount of liquid (water, milk, consommé, gravy, etc.), usually 1/4 cup (60 mL) is sufficient, cover with a glass lid or plastic wrap. Again if your oven has a Sensor or Instamatic Cooking Heat, touch pad 1 or as directed in your microwave manual.

To reheat by time
Cover with waxed paper and heat at MEDIUM-HIGH for 2 to 6 minutes, stirring halfway through heating.

How to defrost chicken, other birds and game

To cook a frozen chicken to perfection, it must first be defrosted completely. Personally, I favor slow defrosting by placing the chicken in a dish and letting it stand in the refrigerator without unwrapping, for 12 to 24 hours. This allows the flesh to slacken and excess moisture is easily removed. Of course, emergencies do arise with insufficient time for this type of slow defrosting. That is when your microwave oven comes to the rescue!

1. Remove chicken (cut-up or whole) from original wrapper.
2. Place a Microwave-safe rack in the bottom of a dish. Set the chicken or cut-up chicken on it. Do not cover.
3. Set DEFROST. A whole chicken up to 4 pounds (2 kg) will require 12 to 14 minutes per pound (24 to 28 minutes per kg).
   A cut-up chicken, 8 to 10 minutes per pound (16 to 20 minutes per kg).
   A boned chicken breast, 10 to 12 minutes per pound (20 to 24 minutes per kg).
4. **IMPORTANT:** The whole chicken or cut-up chicken must be turned over three to four times during defrosting.
5. As soon as possible, break apart the chicken pieces before completion of the DEFROST cycle.
6. As the chicken or cut-up chicken is removed from the microwave oven, rinse under cold water.
   My favorite method consists in washing the defrosted chicken or cut-up chicken with a cloth soaked in either fresh lemon juice, white wine, sherry or brandy. Whatever liquid is used, do not wipe after moistening. Spread the pieces or set the chicken on a sheet of absorbent paper and let stand 20 to 30 minutes before cooking.

Auto Weight Defrost

Some ovens feature a defrost system referred to as Auto Weight Defrost. Another wonder of microwave **ovens**. Read the instructions given in your oven manual for Auto Weight Defrost. The defrosting is automatic. It is used to defrost many cuts of meat, poultry and fish, whole or cut-up, frankfurters, etc. The following applies to all types of auto weight defrost.

- Remove wrapper because the wrap will hold steam and juice close to the food, which can sometimes cause the outer surface of the food to cook.
- I like to place the meat on a microwave safe rack set in a dish. Then, I simply set the control.
- **Chicken and other birds** — Set breast-side down on rack.
- **Ground Meat** — Remove from wrapping or freezing dish. Set on rack.
- **After Defrosting** — Read instructions given in your oven manual. e.g. whole poultry may still be icy in the center. Run cold water in to cavity. If the giblets are inside, they will then be easily removed.
- **Small items,** such as chops, shrimp, cornish hens, etc., can stand 10 to 20 minutes after defrosting.
- **Large Roast** — If still icy in the middle, let stand 30 to 40 minutes, covered with a sheet of waxed paper.

How to test the doneness of a chicken

In a properly cooked chicken the breast will be white throughout showing no brilliant spot when sliced. The brown meat will slice easily and show no tinge of pink.

A chicken should never be cooked rare. On the other hand, overcooking chicken leaves it dry and tasteless.

Each of the following recipes gives a specific cooking time, but since wattage varies in Microwaves, cooking periods may vary (see comparative chart on page...), here is the way to test the doneness of birds.

A. **With a meat thermometer.** Stop the oven, insert the tip of the thermometer into the thickest part of the white meat, being sure it does not touch bones, which would give a higher reading. Poultry is done at 180° - 185°F (82° - 85°C).
B. **By touch.** Test lightly with thumb and index finger. If cooked it will have a springy feel, slightly resistant to indentation.
C. Try moving the leg bone; when cooked it is even possible to pull it off.

Types of poultry and game

There are many reasons why chicken is a year round favorite. It is easy to prepare; easy on the budget; it can be served in dozens of ways, elegant, gourmet, simple. I think the only dilemma chicken poses for those who enjoy cooking is the question of what type to buy. The answer is easy if you know how you wish to prepare it and how many people you will be serving.

I usually allow half a pound (250 g) per serving. The type of chicken you choose indicates the age and approximate size, so choose one that meets your specific needs.

- **Broiler-fryers** are all-purpose chickens, ideal for frying, roasting, stewing. They are about nine weeks old and weigh from 2 to 4 pounds (1 to 2 kg).
- **Roasters** are your best choice for roast chicken or roast stuffed chicken. Larger than broiler-fryers, they are about twelve weeks old and weigh 3½ to 5 pounds (1.75 to 2.5 kg).
- **Capons** are "deluxe" chickens, they have more white meat than other chickens and are very tender. Usually roasted, these young desexed male chickens weigh from 4 to 7 pounds (2 to 3.5 kg). When a large chicken salad is needed for a buffet or special party, they are the best buy, as they offer the most meat for the same price as a good chicken.
- **Cornish hens,** sometimes called game hens, are the smallest members of the chicken family. They are delicate, tasty and elegant. They weigh from 1 to 2 pounds (500 g to 1 kg), usually a one-pound (500 g) bird is used for each serving, the 2-pound (1 kg) one is cut in half. They are at their best when stuffed and roasted. They are often cooked or served with fresh fruit.
- **Turkeys,** the young females of 10 to 14 pounds (5 to 7 kg) are the best for flavor and texture. The best weight for roasting turkey in the   Microwave is from 8 to 13 pounds (4 to 6,5 kg).
- **A Goose** should weigh between 10 and 14 pounds (5 to 7 kg) to be at its best. Heavier types are very fat.

We also have game farms in operation, which all year round produce ducks, quail, pheasant, etc., sold fresh or frozen.

Chicken is an excellent meat, and a source of high quality protein, niacin and iron. One very interesting point is that 3½ ounces (88 g) of white chicken meat, skinned, contain only 166 calories. Furthermore, pricewise, chicken is a very good buy, and very easy to cook in the Microwave. Whichever way you choose to cook your poultry or small game, from roasted to poached, the Microwave makes it simple and ensures success. Microwave oven selections include "Convection", "Sensor", "Cook-by-Weight", etc., depending on your type of Microwave. Of prime importance is to read your oven manual carefully so as to clearly understand all the possibilities which your Microwave offers.

Chicken

Poached Chicken

A classic French cuisine recipe which I have adapted very successfully to Microwave cooking. The cooked chicken may be served with a sauce of your choice (see Sauce Chapter), or made into a pie or salad or simply sliced. The very concentrated broth makes excellent soup.

2 medium carrots, thinly sliced

1 medium onion, sliced

1 medium leek, minced

2 celery stalks, diced

3 tbsp. (50 mL) butter

2 bay leaves

1 tsp. (5 mL) tarragon

1/2 tsp. (2 mL) thyme

6 sprigs of parsley, minced

1 tbsp. (15 mL) coarse salt

1/2 tsp. (2 mL) freshly ground pepper

3 lb (1.5 kg) chicken parts or
A 3 to 4-lb (1.5 to 2 kg) chicken

1 cup (250 mL) white wine (optional)

2 cups (500 mL) chicken broth

In a 14-cup (3.5 L) casserole-dish, place the carrots, onion, leek, celery, butter, bay leaves, tarragon, thyme, parsley, salt and pepper. Stir together. Cover and cook 10 minutes at HIGH. Stir well. The vegetables are then glossy and have lost their firmness. Add the chicken pieces or whole chicken, covering them here and there with the vegetables. Add 1/4 cup (60 mL) of wine or chicken broth. Cover and cook at HIGH 20 to 25 minutes or until the chicken is tender. Stir together twice during the cooking period, allowing the chicken to absorb all the flavor from the vegetables and herbs. Add the remaining wine and the chicken broth. Cook at HIGH 5 minutes. Serve directly from the casserole dish or cool in its juice, strain and use as you wish.

Small Broiler, Ivory Sauce

The perfect recipe to cook a small 2½ to 3-lb (1 to 1.5 kg) broiler. It is also the recipe to follow when you wish to steam any type of small bird. Excellent if you are on a diet as you may simply reduce the butter and omit the cream. Also recommended when you wish to serve creamed chicken in a pie or in puff pastry shells.

A 2½ to 3-lb (1 to 1.5 kg) chicken
1 tsp. (5 mL) salt
1/2 tsp. (2 mL) pepper
2 tbsp. (30 mL) butter
1 leek or large onion, sliced
1 medium carrot, sliced
1/2 cup (125 mL) diced celery
1/2 cup (125 mL) water
1/4 tsp. (1 mL) thyme
1/2 tsp. (2 mL) tarragon

Ivory sauce :
3 tbsp. (50 mL) butter
1/4 cup (60 mL) flour*
The broth from the cooked chicken
1/3 cup (80 mL) light cream
Enough milk to measure 2 cups (500 mL)

Place the salt and pepper in the chicken cavity. Fold wings under and tie legs together.
Melt the 2 tablespoons (30 mL) butter in a dish** large enough to take the chicken. Add the leek or onion, the carrot and the celery. Cook 4 minutes at HIGH, stir well, add the water, thyme and tarragon. Stir well and place the prepared chicken breast-side down in the dish. Cover. Cook at HIGH 10 minutes. Baste chicken, then cook at MEDIUM-HIGH 3 minutes per pound (500 g). Turn chicken breast-side up, after the first 3 minutes.
Ivory Sauce : Melt 3 tablespoons (50 mL) butter in a 4-cup (1 L) measuring cup. Add the flour, stir well and add the drained bouillon from the cooked chicken. Stir, add the cream and enough milk for 2 cups. Stir and cook at HIGH 2 minutes, stir well and repeat cooking if sauce is not sufficiently cooked. Salt and pepper to taste. Pour over the chicken and vegetables. Stir well and serve.

* I like to use Instant Flour, which gives a creamier and lighter sauce, but any flour will do.
** I use à ''Micro-Dur'' dish of 300 mL (marked under dish) with an airtight cover.

Milk Fried Chicken

A delight of my youth, an old-fashioned way to brown and cook a chicken, then finish it in milk sauce. My mother served it with hot buttered French bread and a bowl of minced chives or parsley which we used as we liked.
This recipe is proof that even old traditional recipes can be adapted to Microwave cooking.

A 3-lb (1.5 kg) chicken	1/4 tsp. (1 mL) turmeric
1/4 cup (60 mL) flour	2 tbsp. (30 mL) butter or bacon fat
2 tsp. (10 mL) salt	3 tbsp. (50 mL) flour
1/4 tsp. (1 mL) pepper	2 cups (500 mL) milk

Cut the chicken into individual pieces. Wipe with absorbent paper. Mix together the flour, salt, pepper and turmeric. Roll each piece of chicken in this mixture until well coated.
Melt the butter or bacon fat in an 8 x 8-inch dish (20 x 20 cm), 5 minutes at HIGH; the butter will brown, but the bacon fat will be very hot. Place the chicken pieces skin-side down in the fat. Brown 8 to 10 minutes at HIGH, turn pieces, cook at MEDIUM-HIGH 8 to 10 minutes. Remove chicken to a warm dish. Cover and let stand while making the sauce.
Add the flour to the fat in the dish, mix well, scraping brown pieces. Add the milk, mix well. Cook 4 to 6 minutes at HIGH, stirring twice. When creamy, salt, pepper to taste, and pour over the chicken. Serve.

Chicken Teriyaki

It takes a lot of experience and a serious knowledge of Japanese food to be able to cook in the true perfection of their cuisine. The following recipe is an adaptation, but a good one, and easy to prepare.

3 lb (1.5 kg) chicken breast or chicken legs	1 large garlic clove, chopped fine
1/2 cup (125 mL) soy sauce*	1 tbsp. (15 mL) dark brown sugar
1 tsp. (5 mL) sesame oil	1 tbsp. (15 mL) freshly grated ginger root
1/4 cup (60 mL) Sake or dry sherry	

Wash chicken, place it in plastic bag. Mix the remaining ingredients and pour over the chicken. If you place the bag in a bowl, it is easy to pour in the liquid. Tie the bag and stir all around so the chicken is coated with the marinade. Refrigerate 2 to 8 hours.
To cook, remove chicken from bag, reserving the marinade. Place the chicken in an oblong dish. Cover the tip of the legs with little pieces of aluminum foil. Cook 15 minutes at HIGH, baste generously with the marinating liquid. Cook another 10 minutes at MEDIUM. Let stand 5 minutes. Serve with plain boiled rice.
Add the remaining marinade to the gravy, heat at HIGH 1 minute.
Serve as a sauce, to pour over the chicken and the rice.

* Use Kikkoman Soy Sauce when available; it is lighter and milder than the Chinese soy sauce.

Chicken "Montagnais"

I was taught how to make this chicken by an old shepherd in the French Alps. Simple, unusual and interesting.

A 2 to 4-lb chicken (1 to 2 kg)

3 slices of dry bread

A large clove of unpeeled garlic

1/4 cup (60 mL) minced parsley

The grated rind of 1 lemon

1/2 tsp. (2 mL) salt

1/4 tsp. (1 mL) pepper

1 tbsp. (15 mL) soft butter

2 tsp. (10 mL) vegetable oil

1 tsp. (5 mL) paprika

The Sauce :

2 tbsp. (30 mL) butter

2 tbsp. (30 mL) flour

1 small onion, chopped fine

1 clove garlic, chopped fine

1/2 cup (125 mL) chicken bouillon

1/2 cup (125 mL) white wine or cream

1/4 tsp. (1 mL) tarragon

Wrap a paper towel around 2 slices of bread. Place in the Microwave on a rack. Cook at HIGH 1 minute, touch the bread to see if it is dry. If necessary, cook another 30 seconds to 1 minute. Cool 1 minute. Cut a small slice at the end of the clove of garlic and rub hard on the dried bread. The garlic will melt into the bread. Dice the bread.

Mix the parsley, lemon rind, salt and pepper. Add the diced bread, mix and stuff into the chicken. Secure the opening with toothpicks. Blend together the butter, oil and paprika. Rub all over the chicken with your hands. Pour remaining mixture, if any, on top of chicken. Place chicken on a rack set on a dish, breast-side down. Cook 10 minutes per pound (500 g) at MEDIUM-HIGH. After 15 minutes of cooking, place chicken breast-side up and finish the cooking period as needed depending on the weight of the chicken. When done, remove chicken to a hot platter. Cover and keep warm.

To make the sauce, mix the butter and flour, add to the chicken gravy, mix well, add the remaining ingredients. Stir and cook at HIGH 3 minutes, stir well and cook another 3 minutes. Taste for seasoning, serve in a sauceboat. I like to pour a few tablespoons of this creamy sauce over the chicken before serving.

Lemon Chicken Barcelona *(photo front cover)*

A lemon-steamed chicken with a delicious light gravy. Serve with small dumplings cooked in chicken stock, or with rice stirred with parsley and toasted almonds.

A 3-lb (1.5 kg) broiler	1/2 tsp. (2 mL) paprika
1 tsp. (5 mL) salt	1 lemon, unpeeled, thinly sliced
1/2 tsp. (2 mL) pepper	3 tbsp. (50 mL) butter

Wash chicken, wipe as dry as possible.
Mix the salt, pepper and paprika. Rub chicken all over with the mixture. Fill cavity with the slices of lemon. Tie legs together. Close cavity.
Place the butter in an 8 x 8-inch (20 x 20 cm) dish. Heat at HIGH 3 to 4 minutes or until butter is browned. Place chicken breast-side down in browned butter. Cook at HIGH 10 minutes. Turn chicken. Baste with drippings. Cook at MEDIUM 10 minutes, test for doneness, if necessary cook another 5 minutes. Remove chicken to a hot platter. Add a few spoonfuls of hot water or chicken broth to the juice in the pan. Heat at HIGH 1 minute. Stir well. Pour over chicken or serve in sauceboat.

Norwegian "Citron" Chicken *(first photo)*

A very interesting cold chicken, the perfect buffet dish. In Norway, they surround it with steamed prawn or lobster, but the chicken by itself is tasty and interesting.

6 cups (1.5 L) hot water	3 tbsp. (50 mL) flour
A 3-lb (1.5 kg) chicken	1 cup (250 mL) light cream
1 tsp. (5 mL) coarse salt	2 tbsp. (30 mL) dry sherry
15 peppercorns	Salt, pepper, to taste
6 to 8 celery leaves tied together	2 tbsp. (30 mL) grated lemon rind
8 to 10 parsley stems tied together	***
1/2 tsp. (2 mL) thyme	2 cups (500 mL) shredded lettuce or watercress
***	1 lb (500 kg) cooked shrimp or lobster meat (optional)
3 egg yolks	

Place the first 7 ingredients in an 8-cup saucepan (2 L). Cover. Cook at HIGH 30 to 40 minutes or until chicken is tender. Remove from oven. Let stand until cool or 4 to 5 hours. Remove chicken from the bouillon. Remove and discard the skin. Slice all the meat. Set on an attractive serving dish.
Beat the egg yolks with the flour, cream and sherry. Add the lemon rind. Cook 10 minutes at MEDIUM, beat with a whisk, if necessary, cook 2 to 5 minutes at MEDIUM-HIGH or until creamy. Salt and pepper to taste. Stir well. While hot, pour over the chicken set on the serving dish. Refrigerate overnight.
To serve, surround the dish with shredded lettuce or watercress. If you wish place pieces of cooked seafood over the lettuce.

Glazed Roasted Chicken

The liquid glaze brushed over the chicken before cooking gives the skin a delicious flavor. It is an old French method which I have adapted to the Microwave.

A 3 to 4-lb (1.5 to 2 kg) chicken

1 onion, chopped

3 unpeeled lemon slices

1 celery stalk

1 tsp. (2 mL) thyme

The Glaze:

3 tbsp. (50 mL) butter

1½ tsp. (7 mL) paprika

1 tsp. (5 mL) Kitchen Bouquet

1/4 tsp. (1 mL) thyme or tarragon

The gravy:

2 tbsp. (30 mL) Madeira or port or cold tea

Salt and pepper to taste

Tie the chicken legs and wings as usual. Place a microwave-safe rack in an 8 x 10-inch (20 x 25 cm) dish. Prepare the glaze. Place the butter, paprika, Kitchen Bouquet and thyme in a measuring cup and heat 1 minute at HIGH. Fill the chicken cavity with the lemon slices, celery and thyme.
Mix the glaze thoroughly and brush all over the chicken.
Put the chicken on the rack breast-side down. Cook 7 minutes per pound (14 minutes per kg) at HIGH, turning it halfway through the cooking. Baste with the juice in the pan and finish cooking. Let stand 8 to 10 minutes. Place on a warm dish. Add the Madeira, port or cold tea. Stir well and heat 1 minute at HIGH. Serve in a sauce-boat.

Crisp Quartered Chicken *(photo page 32-33)*

I roast this chicken in the Microwave, cut into quarters, which I sometimes replace by a few pounds of chicken wings or 6 to 8 chicken legs.
I recommend using the "Flavored Breadcrumbs" which are economical and very tasty.*

1 cup (250 mL) homemade coating**

A 3-lb (1.5 kg) chicken, cut in four

1 egg white, lightly beaten

1 tsp. (5 mL) cold water or white wine

3 tbsp. (50 mL) melted butter

Place the coating of your choice on a square of waxed paper.
In a large plate, beat together with a fork, the egg white, cold water or wine.
Roll the pieces of chicken in the egg white-water mixture, then into the coating, until every part of the chicken is well covered. Place the chicken pieces one next to the other in a glass or ceramic baking dish.
Melt the butter 1 minute at HIGH.
Spoon all over the chicken pieces. Roast at HIGH 10 minutes and 5 minutes at MEDIUM. Let stand 10 minutes and serve, as is or with Lemon Caper Sauce, which you will find in the Sauce Chapter.

* *See recipe in Sauce chapter.*
** *A commercial coating may be used, if you wish.*

31

Crisp Quartered Chicken
(page 31)

Chicken Breasts

Chicken Madeira

A classic recipe of Portuguese cuisine. Try to use Portuguese Madeira wine, as it gives a beautiful flavor and color to the dish.

3 tbsp. (50 mL) butter

**3 French shallots, minced or
   6 green onions, chopped fine**

1/2 lb (500 g) fresh mushrooms, sliced

1 tsp. (5 mL) tarragon

Salt and pepper to taste

1/4 cup (60 mL) dry Madeira wine

6 to 8 boneless chicken breasts

Melt the butter 1 minute at HIGH in a dish large enough to hold the chicken breasts in one layer. Add the shallots or green onions. Heat at MEDIUM 3 minutes. Stir well, add the mushrooms and tarragon. Stir well, heat at HIGH 2 minutes. Stir and add salt and pepper to taste and the Madeira wine. Heat at HIGH 2 minutes.

Place each breast on a wooden board or between waxed paper. Pound with a mallet to thin them out. Roll each breast, tie with thread and place it in the hot sauce in the dish. Cook at MEDIUM-HIGH 15 minutes. Test with a fork for doneness. If necessary, heat another 3 to 5 minutes. Remove from oven. Set on serving dish, keep warm. Pour gravy remaining in dish over the chicken.

Chicken Breasts Autumn Leaves

A stuffing of nuts and apples gives an autumn air to this chicken dish.

4 chicken breasts, boned, cut in half
2 cups (500 mL) diced crustless bread
1 tsp. (5 mL) tarragon or thyme
1 tsp. (5 mL) salt
1/4 tsp. (1 mL) pepper
1/2 tsp. (2 mL) crushed garlic
1/3 cup (80 mL) chopped walnuts or pecans
1/2 cup (125 mL) sultana raisins
3 tbsp. (50 mL) melted butter
2 apples, peeled and grated
1/2 cup (125 mL) apple juice
Grated rind of 1 lemon
3 tbsp. (50 mL) soft butter

The Sauce:
1 small onion, chopped fine
1 tsp. (5 mL) butter
1 cup (250 mL) thinly sliced mushrooms
1 tbsp. (15 mL) flour
3 tbsp. (50 mL) brandy or Madeira wine
2/3 cup (160 mL) cream

Wipe the boneless chicken breasts with a cloth dipped in port wine or orange juice.
Mix all the remaining ingredients except the last 3 tablespoons (50 mL) of butter. Blend thoroughly to make a sort of paste. Divide evenly on the chicken half breasts, forming a little roll in the middle of each. Roll and secure each piece of chicken with toothpicks. Roll each one lightly in flour (1 tbsp. — 15 mL), stirred with 1 tsp. (5 mL) paprika.
Preheat a browning dish 6 minutes at HIGH. Rub each piece of chicken with the remaining
3 tablespoons (50 mL) soft butter.
Place the rolls in the browning dish without removing it from the oven. Cook at HIGH 8 minutes. Turn rolls over, cook at MEDIUM-HIGH 6 to 7 minutes. Let stand 5 minutes. Set rolls on a hot platter.
To make the sauce: Add the onion to the fat in the dish. Add the butter, the sliced mushrooms. Stir well. Cook 3 minutes at HIGH. Add the flour and mix well. Add the brandy or Madeira wine and the cream of your choice. Stir. Heat at HIGH 3 to 4 minutes. Stir well and pour over the chicken.

Chicken Breasts Milano *(photo page 16-17)*

A specialty of Italian cuisine, which I find even better when cooked in the Microwave. When I serve it hot, I top the chicken with a mushroom sauce. If I serve it cold, I omit the sauce. I slice the cold stuffed breast which I set around a rice salad; the green of the spinach is very colorful.

4 whole chicken breasts, boned

Stuffing:

Salt, pepper to taste

A package of fresh spinach

1/2 cup (125 mL) fine breadcrumbs

1/2 tsp. (2 mL) savory

1 tsp. (5 mL) basil

1 egg

1/4 cup (60 mL) soft butter

6 green onions, chopped fine

1 large garlic clove, chopped fine

Seasoned sherry:

1/4 tsp. (1 mL) salt

1/4 cup (60 mL) dry sherry

1/4 cup (60 mL) melted butter

1 tsp. (5 mL) paprika

Sauce:

2 tbsp. (30 mL) butter

2 tsp. (10 mL) cornstarch

1/4 cup (60 mL) cream or milk

1/2 lb (250 g) sliced fresh mushrooms

Salt and pepper the inside of the chicken breasts. Pour boiling water on the spinach (remove hard stems when washing them). Let stand 10 minutes, drain thoroughly, chop. Add the next 7 ingredients. Mix well. Spread mixture equally over the inside of each breast. Roll, tie with wooden picks. Place in a Corning pie plate, breast-side up. Blend together the ingredients for the seasoned sherry.

Cook chicken breasts 15 minutes at HIGH. Pour a teaspoon (5 mL) of seasoned sherry over each breast. Cook at MEDIUM another 10 minutes. Let stand covered 10 minutes.

To make the sauce: Melt the butter 1 minute at HIGH. Blend in the cornstarch and add the cream or milk. Cook 3 minutes at HIGH. Stir once while cooking. Add the mushrooms and any of the drippings from the cooking of the chicken breast. Cook at MEDIUM-HIGH 3 to 4 minutes. Stir well and serve separately.

Chicken Breasts "Soubise"

Soubise means onions. And the chicken breasts do cook on a bed of onions flavored with white vermouth. Serve with fine parsleyed noodles or buttered rice.

2 large onions, sliced into rings

1/2 tsp. (2 mL) salt

4 chicken breast halves

3 tbsp. (50 mL) soft butter

1/4 tsp. (1 mL) each pepper and thyme

1 tsp. (5 mL) paprika

1/4 cup (60 mL) white vermouth

2 tbsp. (30 mL) cream of your choice

Place the onion rings in the bottom of an 8 x 8-inch (20 x 20 cm) ceramic or "Micro-Dur" dish. Shape the breasts nicely and place one in each corner of the dish. Mix together the soft butter, pepper, thyme and paprika. Spread this butter over the top of each breast, preferably with your fingers.

Cook uncovered 10 minutes at HIGH. Remove the breasts from the dish without turning them. Add the vermouth and stir well. Heat 3 minutes at HIGH.

Return the breasts to the dish. Cover and cook at HIGH 10 minutes. Set the chicken on a warm serving dish.

Add the cream to the sauce. Beat with a metal whisk or an electric beater. Taste for seasoning. Heat at HIGH 2 minutes. Pour over the chicken breasts or all around.

Glazed Chicken Breasts, Country Inn

Alain Chapel, Three-Star Chef, created this recipe. He was amused by my adaptation of his recipe to Microwave cooking, and he strongly encouraged me to add it to the other recipes. His tomato "coulis" is superb. It may also be served with a roast of veal or poached sole fillets.

Tomato "coulis":

4 red tomatoes

3 tbsp. (50 mL) olive oil

1 garlic clove, unpeeled, cut in two

2 tsp. (10 mL) sugar

Chicken:

2 chicken breasts, cut in two

Salt, pepper and paprika, to taste

2 tsp. (10 mL) red wine vinegar

1 tbsp. (15 mL) Japanese or white wine vinegar

2 tsp. (10 mL) Dijon mustard

1/4 cup (60 mL) white wine or white vermouth

3 tbsp. (50 mL) tomato "coulis"

1 tsp. (5 mL) butter

Cut the tomatoes in four. Heat the oil in a baking dish 1 minute at HIGH. Add the unpeeled garlic, stir in the oil and brown lightly 2 minutes at HIGH. Stir, add the tomatoes and sugar, cook 5 minutes at HIGH. Stir well and cook at HIGH 4 or 5 minutes or until the tomatoes have lost most of their juice and have a somewhat creamy texture. Put through a fine sieve.

Cut each breast in two, you will then have four pieces. Preheat a browning dish, 6 minutes at HIGH. Sprinkle each piece of chicken with salt, pepper and paprika. Place the chicken pieces skin-side down in the hot dish, without removing it from the oven. Brown 5 minutes at HIGH. Turn the chicken, pour the red wine vinegar on top. Cook 4 minutes at HIGH. In the meantime, mix together the Dijon mustard, white wine or vermouth and tomato "coulis". Set chicken on a hot serving dish. Add the above mustard mixture to the juice in the baking dish. Mix well. Cook 3 minutes at HIGH. Stir, add the butter and mix thoroughly. Pour over the chicken.

If the chicken has cooled, it is easy to reheat by placing the serving dish in the microwave 3 to 5 minutes at MEDIUM. Serve with a bowl of rice.

Portuguese Glazed Chicken Breast

Chicken "nouvelle cuisine", a very lengthy preparation on top of the stove, but quick and easy in the Microwave. The perfect dish for an elegant dinner, served with fine green noodles or asparagus.

2 tbsp. (30 mL) butter

4 chicken breast halves

1 cup (250 mL) leeks, thinly sliced

2 French shallots, minced

1 bunch watercress or parsley, whole

1/3 cup (80 mL) port wine

2/3 cup (160 mL) chicken broth

2 egg yolks

3 tbsp. (50 mL) cold water

Salt and pepper

Melt the butter in the baking dish 1 minute at HIGH.
Add the leeks and shallots. Stir well. Cook 4 minutes at MEDIUM-HIGH, stirring halfway through cooking. Add the watercress or parsley, the port and chicken broth. Heat uncovered 3 minutes at HIGH. Stir. Roll up each half breast like a sausage.
Salt and pepper to taste. Place the chicken in the port sauce and baste. Cover with lid or plastic wrap. Cook 18 minutes at MEDIUM. Let stand 10 minutes. Remove breasts to a hot serving plate. Pour the hot sauce mixture into the processor or blender bowl. Add the egg yolks beaten lightly with the cold water. Cover and beat to obtain a creamy sauce. Pour into a dish and cook 2 minutes at HIGH, stirring well after 1 minute. You will then have a lovely green sauce. Pour over the chicken breast. Reheat 2 minutes at MEDIUM. Serve.

Chicken Breasts or Legs California

Chicken breasts, cooked over a bed of melted onions, served with a creamy sauce and parsleyed rice. I sometimes replace the breast by chicken legs, more economical and just as easy to make.

2 good-sized chicken breasts, boneless, or 6 to 8 chicken legs

1/2 to 3/4 cup (125 - 190 mL) onion, thinly sliced

1/4 cup (60 mL) butter or margarine

1/2 tsp. (2 mL) thyme or tarragon

3 thin slices of unpeeled lemon

1/3 cup (80 mL) heavy or light cream

Salt, pepper to taste

1 tbsp. (15 mL) flour

I prefer to cut each chicken breast in half. When time permits I bone the chicken legs and turn them into neat rolls, but they can also be cooked whole.

Melt the butter or margarine, 3 minutes at HIGH in a dish large enough to hold the chosen type of chicken, the pieces one next to the other. Add the onions, thyme or tarragon and lemon slices to the melted butter. Stir well. Cook at HIGH 3 minutes, stirring once. This will soften the onions.

Stir well and place the pieces of chicken over the onions. Pour the cream over all. Salt, pepper to taste. Cover the dish with a lid or plastic wrap. Cook at MEDIUM-HIGH 20 minutes for the chicken breasts, 25 to 28 minutes for the chicken legs. Remove dish from Microwave and place chicken on a warm platter. Strain the onions from the liquid with a perforated spoon. Place them over the chicken.

To the liquid left in the pan, add the flour, mix well and add the cream. Stir, cook 4 minutes at MEDIUM-HIGH, stirring after 2 minutes. Salt and pepper to taste. Pour over the chicken and onions.

Chicken Pieces

Baked Chicken La Jolla

I ate this chicken in California, enjoying it thoroughly, so I adapted it to Microwave cooking.

2½ to 3 lb (1 to 1.5 kg) chicken pieces

1 tsp. (5 mL) basil

The rind of half a lemon

1/2 tsp. (2 mL) freshly ground pepper

6 green onions, chopped fine

The juice of half a lemon and half an orange

1/2 tsp. (2 mL) crushed or powdered coriander seeds (optional)

1/2 tsp. (2 mL) paprika

Pat chicken pieces with a paper towel, as dry as possible.
Place on a piece of waxed paper the basil, pepper and lemon rind. Rub mixture into the chicken parts.
Arrange chicken in a Microwave 10-inch (25 cm) round dish, placing small parts like the drumsticks toward the middle of the dish.
Sprinkle chopped green onions on top. Combine the lemon and orange juice, the coriander seeds and the paprika. Pour over the chicken, cover, cook 10 minutes at HIGH. Baste chicken with juices in the bottom of the dish. Cook 12 to 15 minutes at MEDIUM-HIGH. Let stand 5 to 8 minutes, baste with juices after 4 minutes.
Serve with parsleyed rice or green noodles.

Chicken Wings with Bacon

Equally good hot or cold. Always popular. Serve cold on a picnic, or to the men watching baseball or hockey. Serve it with hot buttered French bread.

6 bacon slices

6 chicken wings

2 tbsp. (30 mL) flour

1/2 tsp. (2 mL) paprika

1/2 tsp. (2 mL) savory or thyme

Salt and pepper to taste

1 tbsp. (15 mL) flour

1/2 cup (125 mL) apple juice, water, cream or white wine

Dice bacon. Place in an 8 x 8-inch (20 x 20 cm) Microwave dish. Cook 2 minutes at HIGH.
Combine flour with seasonings. Roll wings in the mixture. Place wings with rounded part down in the hot bacon.
Cook 10 minutes at HIGH. Turn the wings and stir the bacon that sticks to the dish. Continue cooking at MEDIUM 5 minutes or until chicken is tender. Remove wings. Add the 1 tablespoon (15 mL) flour to fat in the dish and stir. Add water or apple juice or the liquid of your choice and stir well. Cook 3 minutes at MEDIUM-HIGH. Pour over the chicken wings.

Boiled Chicken with Dumplings

The chicken may be cooked a few hours ahead of time. It reheats in 15 minutes at MEDIUM. You then remove chicken parts with a perforated spoon, cook the dumplings in the hot liquid, and serve.

The chicken:
A 3-lb (1.5 kg) chicken, cut up or
   3 lb (1.5 kg) chicken legs or wings
2 cups (500 mL) chicken broth
1 large onion, chopped
2 celery stalks with leaves, diced
4 medium carrots, sliced
2 tsp. (10 mL) salt
1/2 tsp. (2 mL) pepper
1/2 tsp. (2 mL) tarragon or savory
1/4 tsp. (1 mL) thyme
1 garlic clove, chopped fine
1/2 cup (125 mL) cold water

Dumplings:
1½ cups (375 mL) flour
1 tsp. (5 mL) dried parsley (optional)
1/4 tsp. (1 mL) savory
2 tsp. (10 mL) baking powder
1/2 tsp. (2 mL) salt
2/3 cup (160 mL) milk
1 egg
2 tbsp. (30 mL) vegetable oil

The chicken: Place all the ingredients in a large 16-cup (4 L) bowl, cover and cook 30 minutes at MEDIUM-HIGH, or until the chicken is tender. Stir well. Remove chicken from broth with a perforated spoon. Cover to keep warm.

Dumplings: Mix together the flour, parsley, savory, baking powder and salt. In another bowl, beat the remaining ingredients together, add to the flour mixture and beat just enough to blend only when ready to cook. Drop by spoonfuls into the broth. Cover and cook 5 minutes at HIGH or until the dumplings are puffed and cooked. Place the cooked dumplings around the chicken. Pour a tablespoon or two (15-30 mL) of the juice over the chicken. Serve.

Orange Marmalade Chicken Wings

Beautifully glazed chicken wings. I sometimes replace the marmalade by homemade apple jelly flavored with orange rind. Serve hot with small parsleyed noodles or cold with a green salad.

8 to 10 chicken wings

2 tbsp. (30 mL) butter

1/2 tsp. (2 mL) tarragon or basil

1 tsp. (5 mL) salt

1/4 tsp. (1 mL) pepper

1/4 tsp. (1 mL) paprika

1/2 cup (125 mL) orange marmalade

The grated rind of 1 orange

Wash wings and dry with paper towelling, tuck the tips under the larger joints to form a triangle. Melt the butter in an 8 x 12-inch (20 x 30 cm) dish 2 minutes at HIGH. Season the wings with the tarragon or basil, salt, pepper and paprika, mixed together. Place in the hot butter, with the small points of wings on top. Cook 10 minutes at HIGH, turn wings over and cook another 6 minutes at HIGH. Spread wings with the orange marmalade or apple jelly mixed with orange rind. Cook another 2 minutes at HIGH. Let stand 5 minutes. Baste 3 times while standing with the juices accumulated in the bottom of the dish. Equally good served hot or cold.

Chicken Wings Dijon

The combination of honey, curry and mustard makes these chicken wings golden brown with an intriguing flavor. Serve with boiled long grain rice mixed with lots of chopped green onions.

2 to 3 lb (1 to 1.5 kg) chicken wings

1 tbsp. (30 mL) Dijon mustard

Juice of 1 lemon or 2 limes

1/2 tsp. (2 mL) curry powder

1/4 tsp. (1 mL) salt

3 tbsp. (50 mL) honey

Place in a dish large enough to hold the chicken wings in one layer, the mustard, lemon or lime juice, curry powder, salt and honey. Cook at HIGH 2 minutes. Roll each chicken wing, folded in a triangle, in the hot mixture. Place wings one next to the other. Cover and cook 10 minutes at MEDIUM-HIGH. Let stand covered 10 minutes before serving.

There will be enough sauce to pour some on each serving of wings.

Chicken Wings Teriyaki

In Japanese cuisine, TERIYAKI implies a mildly sweet soy-base sauce, to be added to lightly grilled meat. TERIYAKI sauce is sold in specialty and food import shops.
The following sauce which I have adapted to Microwave cooking is delicious, and so easy to make. If you wish to make your own TERIYAKI sauce, the following is an interesting formula given to me by a young Japanese girl in Hawai.

Teriyaki Sauce:

7 tbsp. (105 mL) Sake

7 tbsp. (105 mL) mirin (mild wine)

7 tbsp. (105 mL) soy sauce

1 tbsp. (15 mL) sugar

Place all the ingredients in a large measuring cup.
Heat 5 to 6 minutes at HIGH. Stir well. Pour into a glass bottle. Cool and refrigerate. Use as needed.

10 to 12 chicken wings

Paprika

2 tbsp. (30 mL) peanut oil

1 medium onion, thinly sliced

1 celery stalk, diced fine

1/4 cup (60 mL) chili sauce

1/3 cup (80 mL) Teriyaki sauce

Fold the wings. Sprinkle generously with paprika. Heat the peanut oil 2 minutes at HIGH in the baking dish. Add the chicken wings, without removing dish from oven, placing them one next to the other, as much as possible. Stir to coat them with the oil. Cook 6 to 7 minutes at HIGH. Stir the wings. Add the remaining ingredients. Stir thoroughly together. Cook 6 to 8 minutes at HIGH. Stir and serve with rice.

Napa Creamed Chicken
(page 49)

Napa Creamed Chicken *(photo page 48-49)*

Delicious cooked chicken with cream sauce that can be served with rice or with a basket of hot biscuits, or cooked as a pie.

2 tbsp. (30 mL) butter

1/4 cup (60 mL) water or chicken consommé

1 medium onion, chopped

2 carrots, thinly sliced

2 medium potatoes, cut in matchsticks

2 celery stalks, finely diced

2 to 3 cups (500 - 750 mL) diced cooked chicken

The sauce:

3 tbsp. (50 mL) butter

4 tbsp. (60 mL) flour

2½ to 3 cups (625 - 750 mL) chicken consommé

1/2 tsp. (2 mL) dried thyme

1/2 cup (125 mL) fresh parsley, minced, or 3 tbsp. (50 mL) dried parsley

1/4 tsp. (1 mL) nutmeg

Place in a bowl the 2 tablespoons (30 mL) butter and the 1/4 cup (60 mL) chicken consommé, add the onion, carrots, potatoes and celery. Stir well, cover and cook 10 minutes at MEDIUM-HIGH. Stir well, add the diced cooked chicken; stir well, add the thyme, parsley and grated nutmeg. Stir well together, salt and pepper to taste.

Prepare the sauce, by melting the 3 tablespoons (50 mL) butter 2 minutes at HIGH. Add the flour, stir well and add the chicken consommé, stir, cook 4 minutes at HIGH, stir well, cook another 2 minutes at HIGH or until creamy. Stir. Taste for salt and pepper and pour over the chicken. Mix and serve, or cover if prepared ahead of time, but keep on kitchen counter and warm up 6 to 8 minutes at MEDIUM-HIGH, covered, when ready to serve.

Chicken à la King

An old recipe of mine is still the best for using leftover chicken or turkey. Through the years, I have tried many ways of making "Chicken à la King". The following is my favorite recipe, which I find even better when prepared in the Microwave oven.

2 tbsp. (30 mL) butter	3 cups (750 mL) cooked chicken, diced*
1/2 cup (125 mL) diced green pepper	3 egg yolks
1 cup (250 mL) mushrooms, sliced	1/4 tsp. (1 mL) paprika
3 tbsp. (50 mL) flour	3 tbsp. (50 mL) soft butter
2 cups (500 mL) light cream or milk	1 small onion, chopped fine
1/4 tsp. (1 mL) salt	1 tbsp. (15 mL) lemon juice
1/2 tsp. (2 mL) tarragon or	2 tbsp. (30 mL) sherry
1/4 tsp. (1 mL) thyme	

Melt the first 2 tablespoons (30 mL) of butter in a 4-cup (1 L) bowl 1 minute at HIGH. Add the green pepper and the mushrooms, stir well. Cook 3 minutes at HIGH. Push the vegetables to one side, pressing out the butter. Stir the flour into the butter until well blended, then add the cream. Stir with the vegetables until well mixed. Cook 3 minutes at HIGH, stir well and cook another 3 to 6 minutes or until creamy. Salt to taste, add the chicken, mix well, cook 1 minute at HIGH, stir again.

Mix together the egg yolks, paprika, soft butter, onion, lemon juice and sherry. Add to chicken mixture. Stir until well mixed. Cook at MEDIUM 6 to 7 minutes, stirring after 3 minutes. It should be creamy and cooked. Serve in puff pastry shell, or make into a pie, or serve in a nest of cooked rice.

You may use 2 or 3 cups (500 - 750 mL) of cooked chicken, or you may simmer a small 3-pound (1.5 kg) chicken 40 minutes at MEDIUM, cut it and prepare it à la king.

Turkey and Goose

Microwave Roasted Turkey *(photo page 64-65)*

The ideal weight for a Microwave roasted turkey is 8 to 13 pounds (4 to 6.5 kg). My favorite weight is a 10-pound (5 kg) turkey with short stubby legs.

A Microwave-roasted turkey **does** brown, in spite of what many have said. The difference with a Microwave oven-roasted turkey is that the skin has a beautiful colour, but it is not as crisp. Where health is concerned, it is much better, as the hard-to-digest fat does not penetrate the white meat. However, if you do wish to have a crisp browned skin, place the cooked turkey in a roaster, set in a preheated 400°F (200°C) oven. It will take about 10 to 15 minutes for the skin to become crisp. Before placing the turkey in the oven, baste 5 to 6 times with the drippings. But, if you have a combined Microwave-convection oven, place the turkey on the rack in the preheated 400°F (200°C) oven. (See your Oven Manual). The skin will crisp; it may take 10 minutes more than a regular oven.

A 10 to 13-lb (5 to 6.5 kg) turkey

1 tsp. (5 mL) coarse salt

1/4 tsp. (1 mL) pepper

1/2 tsp. (2 mL) nutmeg

1 tsp. (5 mL) tarragon

1/4 cup (60 mL) brandy

1 large onion, cut in half

1 celery stalk

2 garlic cloves, cut in half

1/4 tsp. (1 mL) nutmeg

1/3 cup (80 mL) melted butter

1 tsp. (5 mL) paprika

2 tsp. (10 mL) Kitchen Bouquet

Wash turkey under running cold water. Dry with paper towelling. Mix the salt, pepper, nutmeg, tarragon and brandy. Pour into cavity. Stuff the onion, celery and garlic into the cavity. Push wings under the turkey. Tie legs together with a string. Rub skin all over with the 1/4 teaspoon (1 mL) of nutmeg. Mix the melted butter with paprika and Kitchen Bouquet and brush turkey all over with the mixture. Place breast-side down on a rack. Set in the oven tray or on a dish if tray has no sides to catch the gravy.

Roast at MEDIUM-HIGH 9 minutes per pound (500 g). Turn turkey over. Cover end of legs and top of breast with a small strip of foil wrap, to prevent turkey legs and top of breast from drying. Roast at MEDIUM-HIGH 6 minutes per pound (500 g). Remove foil. Let stand 20 minutes covered with waxed paper, before carving. Inner heat of the cooked turkey should be 180° to 185°F. (80° to 84°C). Check with a meat thermometer.

To Make Gravy: Pour the juices accumulated in the dish into a saucepan or bowl, add 2 tablespoons (30 mL) instant flour or pastry flour, stir well with a whisk, cook at HIGH 2 minutes. Stir again with the whisk and cook at HIGH another minute, stirring once. Add 1/4 cup (60 mL) brandy. Stir well. Microwave another minute or until hot.

NOTE: If you wish to stuff the turkey, look for recipes in the index.

Convection Roasted Turkey

If your Microwave also has the convection method, first read the instructions given in your oven manual, regarding the way to operate the convection part, then follow the recipe given below to roast the turkey. The result will be a crisp browned turkey.

Another advantage is that it can be roasted an hour before being served. Cover hot turkey with a towel topped with foil wrap.

To reheat when ready to serve, uncover, baste all over with drippings and reheat at MEDIUM-LOW 15 minutes.

A 10 to 12-lb (5 to 6 kg) turkey

1 tbsp. (15 mL) butter

1 tbsp. (15 mL) vegetable oil

1 tsp. (5 mL) Dijon or dry mustard

**A large handful of fresh parsley or
celery leaves**

The grated rind of one lemon

1 tsp. (5 mL) summer savory

2 tbsp. (10 mL) coarse salt

1 large onion, cut in four

Wash turkey under cold running water. Dry with paper towelling. Mix together the butter, vegetable oil and mustard. Set aside. Place the remaining ingredients in the cavity. Tie legs together with a string. Fold wings under the turkey. Butter the whole turkey with the butter and oil mixture.

Preheat oven to 375°F. (190°C). Set prepared turkey on low rack. Place a pie plate under the rack to catch the drippings. Cook 12 minutes per pound (500 g) at 375°F. (190°C).

To Make the Gravy: To the juices accumulated in the dish placed under the turkey add 2 tablespoons (30 mL) flour stirred with 1/4 cup (60 mL) chicken consommé. Mix well. Heat at HIGH 2 minutes. Stir, add another 1/4 cup (60 mL) chicken consommé and 1/4 cup (60 mL) port wine or Madeira. Heat 2 minutes at HIGH.

Microwave/Convection Roasted Turkey

Here is a third successful method of cooking a turkey in the Microwave, by alternating Microwave and convection, providing of course, your Microwave also features convection cooking.

An 8 to 14-lb (4 to 7 kg) turkey	**2 tbsp. (30 mL) flour**
1 large garlic clove	**1 tbsp. (15 mL) dry mustard**
Half a lemon	**1 tsp. (5 mL) paprika**
The fat taken from the turkey	**1 tsp. (5 mL) coarse salt**

Wash the turkey and dry it thoroughly. Rub the skin with the garlic clove and the lemon half. Cut the fat into small pieces. Place in a glass or ceramic dish, spread out in the bottom of the dish. Cook at HIGH 2 to 3 minutes, stirring once during the cooking. Remove the browned pieces. Add the flour, mustard and paprika to the fat. Spread this mixture over the turkey breast and legs. Truss the bird. Put the coarse salt in the cavity.

Place the spatter shield, if your oven has one, in the ceramic tray and then the rack. Set the turkey on the rack. Place a pie plate under the rack to catch the drippings. Roast at 350°F (180°C) 10 minutes per pound (500 g). The turkey will cook to perfection. Let stand 15 minutes before serving.

To make the gravy: Remove the turkey from the oven. Place it in a serving dish and cover. Remove the rack and scrape the brown particles from the spatter shield into the pie plate, stirring them into the accumulated fat. Mix thoroughly, add 2 tablespoons (30 mL) of flour, mix into the juices and add 3/4 cup (190 mL) chicken broth or half broth and half wine of your choice or Madeira. Mix thoroughly and cook in the Microwave 2 minutes at HIGH. Stir well. Pour into a sauceboat. If the turkey has cooled, warm up at A1 cycle.

How to Cook a Turkey in a Cooking Bag in the Microwave

A large cooking bag is needed (clear plastic).
- Make sure the turkey is completely defrosted.
- Cover the tips of the wings and legs with strips of aluminum wrap.
- Place inside the turkey a large onion, cut in four, 1 tsp. (5 mL) salt, 1/2 tsp. (2 mL) pepper, 2 bay leaves, 1 tsp. (5 mL) thyme or tarragon.
- Spread the following mixture over the breast, legs and wings:

1/2 cup (125 mL) melted butter

1 tsp. (5 mL) paprika

1/4 tsp. (1 mL) pepper

1/4 tsp. (1 mL) powdered garlic

Mix all the ingredients together. Heat 1 minute at HIGH. Spread this butter over the whole turkey. Place the turkey in the bag, sprinkle with the mixture and tie the bag loosely with a string so the turkey may be moved inside the bag. Place the bag in a 12-cup (3 L) glass cooking dish, breast-side down. Make 4 or 5 slits in the top of the bag. Cook at HIGH 7 to 8 minutes per pound (500 g). Midway through the cooking turn the bag so the breast will be up, continue cooking at MEDIUM-HIGH 8 minutes per pound (500 g). The turkey is cooked when it reaches 160°F (70°C) on the thermometer.

Remove from bag, place on a warm serving dish, cover with a cloth or a paper, let stand, and after 15 minutes the thermometer should register 170°F (75°C).

Meanwhile, make the gravy. Pour into the dish the juice and fat accumulated in the bag. Remove surface fat if you wish. To the juice, add 2 to 3 tablespoons (30 to 50 mL) flour, stir well and add 1/2 cup (125 mL) white wine or cider or chicken broth, according to your taste. Mix well. Cook 4 minutes at HIGH, stir well and, if necessary, cook one more minute for a light and creamy gravy.

Roast Turkey Breast

At our markets we can now find cut-up turkey — either the whole breast, or legs or wings. These are quickly prepared and very tasty. They are usually cut from smaller turkeys. The breast weighs about 2 to 2½ pounds (1 to 1.25 kg), enough to serve up to 4 people.

One turkey breast

3 tbsp. (50 mL) butter or margarine

1 tsp. (5 mL) salt

1/2 tsp. (2 mL) pepper

1 tsp. (5 mL) thyme or sage

1 tbsp. (15 mL) scotch or brandy

1 egg white, lightly beaten

2 tbsp. (30 mL) cold water

2 tbsp. (30 mL) fine dry breadcrumbs

Cream together the butter or margarine, salt, pepper, thyme or sage and scotch or brandy. Spread inside the boned breast, roll and tie loosely with string.
Mix together in a plate the egg white and cold water, and place the dry breadcrumbs on a piece of waxed paper. Roll the breast all over in the egg white mixture, then in the fine breadcrumbs.
Place on a rack. Set rack on a 9-inch (22.5 cm) pie plate. Cook 15 minutes at HIGH, baste lightly with drippings and cook another 8 to 10 minutes at MEDIUM-HIGH or until tender. (Test with a fork or the point of a paring knife).
Serve hot or cold. When served hot, cover and let stand 10 minutes before serving.

Turkey Wings Oriental

Four whole turkey wings will weigh about 4 pounds (2 kg). I cut each wing into two, and I reserve the tips to make turkey stock.

4 whole turkey wings

Paprika

1/3 cup (80 mL) peanut oil

Sauce:

1 cup (250 mL) soy sauce

3 tbsp. (50 mL) Sake or sherry

2 tbsp. (30 mL) grated fresh ginger root

2 garlic cloves, chopped fine

The grated rind of 1 orange and 1 lemon

1 tbsp. (15 mL) brown sugar

Cut each wing into two portions, reserving the wing tips to make stock. Sprinkle each piece with paprika. Dip each part of the wings into the oil. Place in an 8 x 10-inch (20 x 25 cm) dish, the cut part placed toward the middle. Cook 10 minutes at HIGH. Move the pieces around in the dish.
Place the sauce ingredients in a measuring cup. Cook 2 minutes at HIGH. Pour over the turkey wings, cover with waxed paper. Cook at HIGH another 10 minutes. Baste with sauce in the dish. Cover and let rest 10 minutes before serving. Serve with rice.

Scalloped Turkey "à l'Italienne"

Nobody will ever know this is made with leftovers. In Verona, Italy, where I first ate this, the noodles were homemade green noodles, but any type of noodles can be used.

8 oz (250 g) fine noodles

Leftover turkey, sliced or diced, and stuffing

4 tbsp. (60 mL) butter

4 tbsp. (60 mL) flour

1 cup (250 mL) milk

1 cup (250 mL) turkey or chicken broth*

1/4 cup (60 mL) finely chopped parsley

Salt, pepper to taste

3 tbsp. (50 mL) melted butter

3 tbsp. (50 mL) fine breadcrumbs

1/4 tsp. (1 mL) grated nutmeg

Boil the noodles until tender. Drain thoroughly. Place in a casserole, top with sliced or diced turkey, top turkey with leftover stuffing, if any.

Melt butter in a 4-cup (1 L) measure, 1 minute at HIGH. Add the flour, stir well and add the milk and broth. Stir and cook 2 minutes at HIGH. Stir and cook another 2 minutes or until creamy. The time may vary slightly depending on how cold the milk is. Add the parsley, salt and pepper to taste. Pour over the noodles and turkey, until well covered.

Melt the butter 1 minute at HIGH, add the fine breadcrumbs and nutmeg. Mix well and spread over the sauce. Cook 10 minutes at MEDIUM. Serve hot.

* *You can make the broth with the turkey bones.*

Turkey Casserole

It's useful to have good leftover recipes for turkey, as very often we wonder what to do. This **casserole is** a pleasant and tasty family dish.

About 3 cups (750 mL) leftover turkey, sliced or diced

2 tbsp. (30 mL) butter

2 tbsp. (30 mL) flour

1 cup (250 mL) chicken consommé or turkey broth

1 cup (250 mL) cream

2 tbsp. (30 mL) sherry

2 egg yolks, beaten

Buttered breadcrumbs

Melt the butter in a 4-cup (1 L) casserole 1 minute at HIGH. Stir in the flour. Add the chicken consommé or turkey broth. Mix well. Cook at HIGH 2 minutes. Stir well and cook another minute or until creamy.

Add the cream and sherry. Mix well. Stir in the egg yolks. Whisk until well blended with the sauce. Cook at MEDIUM 1 minute. Stir and season to taste.

Place a layer of turkey meat in the bottom of a baking dish, cover with half the sauce, make another layer of turkey meat and top whole with the remaining sauce. Sprinkle buttered breadcrumbs on top. Cover. Cook 8 minutes at MEDIUM. This can be prepared in advance and cooked when ready to serve, simply add 2 minutes cooking time.

Topping variations: Crush 6 soda crackers, add 2 tablespoons (30 mL) melted margarine or butter, 1/2 teaspoon (2 mL) paprika **or** 1 teaspoon (5 mL) sesame seeds, sprinkle on top of casserole and cook the same time as above.

Classic Roasted Goose

I adapted this classic way to roast goose to Microwave cooking. Because of its fat content, the skin was crisp and fat free, the meat, juicy and tender after cooking.
If desired, it may be stuffed with Apple Raisin Stuffing (see Index), or simply seasoned inside the cavity.

A 10 - 12-lb (5 - 6 kg) young goose	6 whole cloves
The juice of 2 lemons	1/2 tsp. (2 mL) thyme
1 onion, thinly sliced	1 tsp. (5 mL) basil
1 large garlic clove, cut in half	1/3 cup (80 mL) parsley stems, chopped

Wipe the goose inside and out with a cloth dipped in vinegar (I like to use cider vinegar). Place the well mixed remaining ingredients in a large bowl and roll the goose all over in the mixture. Cover the bowl with a cloth or with foil and marinate 24 hours, refrigerated or in a cool place.

Then, stuff the bird as you wish or simply put into the cavity 4 unpeeled apples cut in thick slices and the ingredients used to marinate the goose. Tie legs with wooden picks, place wings under the neck skin. Place on a rack set in a Microwave-safe dish large enough to hold the goose. Cover tips of legs with small pieces of foil. Add 2 cups (500 mL) water or apple juice on top of the bird. Sprinkle generously all over with paprika, then rub breast with 2 tablespoons (30 mL) melted butter or margarine, stirred with 1 tablespoon (15 mL) Kitchen Bouquet.

Cover the goose with a large piece of buttered waxed paper. Roast 5 minutes per pound (500 g) at HIGH. Baste with the juice in the bottom of the pan every 20 minutes.

Prick the wings and legs after 40 minutes with the point of a knife to let fat escape. Then continue roasting at MEDIUM-HIGH. Test for doneness with a fork.

To make the gravy, remove goose to a warm platter. Remove excess fat from pan. This is easy as the fat stays on top.

Place in a small bowl, 3 tablespoons (50 mL) of the top clear fat, add 3 to 4 tablespoons (50 - 60 mL) flour. Mix well and cook at MEDIUM-HIGH 3 to 6 minutes, stirring every minute, until mixture reaches a nice brown color. Remove from the roasting dish any fat that remains on top. Add the browned flour mixture to the remaining gravy. Stir well, add 1 cup (250 mL) port wine or orange juice or strong tea. Stir well. Cook 5 minutes at MEDIUM, stirring once; it should then be bubbling and creamy. Serve in a sauce-boat. Excellent served with Port Wine Jelly or English Tart Applesauce (see Index).

Duck

Duck "à l'orange"

This recipe is suitable for wild as well as domestic duck. The only difference is that the wild duck must be tested often for doneness, because cooking time will vary according to age and type of duck.

One 4 to 4.5-lb (2 to 2.5 kg) domestic duck	**2 medium apples, unpeeled**
Juice of 1 lemon	**1 garlic clove**
1 tsp. (5 mL) salt	**8 to 10 peppercorns**
1 tbsp. (15 mL) brown sugar	**1 slice of bread**
The rind of one orange	

Clean the duck inside and outside with the lemon juice. Salt inside the cavity. Mix together the brown sugar, apples cut into eighths, orange rind, garlic and peppercorns. Stuff the cavity with the mixture and close it with the slice of bread. Tie the legs with a wet string. Wrap the tips of the wings and legs with strips of foil.

Place the duck, breast-side down, over an inverted saucer or a Microwave rack, either one placed in the baking dish. Cook 20 minutes at HIGH. Turn the duck on its back.

Cover with waxed paper and roast 20 minutes at MEDIUM-HIGH. Test doneness. It is sometimes necessary to cook 5 minutes more. Put the duck on a serving dish, cover with a bowl or waxed paper and let stand 15 minutes. In the meantime, prepare the orange sauce.

The sauce:	**2/3 cup (160 mL) orange juice**
2 tbsp. (30 mL) brown sugar	**3 tbsp. (50 mL) the brown part of the gravy**
1 tbsp. (15 mL) cornstarch	**3 tbsp. (50 mL) brandy**
Rind of one orange	

Mix together in a large measuring cup or a bowl, the brown sugar and the cornstarch, add to it the orange rind and juice. Strain the drippings. Remove the fat on top and add the brown juice to the orange juice mixture. Mix thoroughly and cook 4 minutes at HIGH, stirring once or twice. Add the brandy and serve.

Plum Sauce Duck
Roasted by convection

The easiest of all ways to cook wild or domestic duck. Serve with boiled rice stirred with diced cooked beets, green onions and finely chopped parsley. The pinkish color of the rice is attractive. The mixture of flavors is interesting with duck.

A 3 to 4-lb (1 kg 500 - 2 kg) duck

A medium-sized onion cut in four

1 unpeeled orange, cut in four

1/2 cup (125 mL) Oriental plum sauce

1 garlic clove, chopped fine

Salt, pepper to taste

Grated rind and juice of 1 orange

1 tsp. (5 mL) sugar

1 tsp. (5 mL) cornstarch

3 tbsp. (50 mL) red wine or port

Rinse duck under cold running water. Dry inside and out with paper towel. Place the onion and orange wedges in duck cavity. Tie legs over the cavity, with a string.
Preheat convection part of your Microwave oven to 375°F (190°C). Place low rack in the oven. Set a Pyrex or ceramic plate under rack to catch the dripping. Blend together, the plum sauce and all the remaining ingredients.
Roll duck in the mixture, pouring a few spoonfuls of it into the cavity. Place duck on rack in preheated oven. Roast 1 hour to 1 hour 15 minutes, basting twice, with some of the drippings in the plate. Let stand 15 minutes before serving.
To make the sauce: Mix 1 teaspoon (5 mL) cornstarch with 3 tablespoons (50 mL) of red wine or port wine. Add to gravy in the plate. Stir well. Cook at HIGH 2 minutes, stir until creamy. Serve.

Microwave Roasted Turkey
(page 53)

Chinese Duck
(Convection)

The following recipe is an adaptation of the lacquered duck. This one is cut-up, but the Chinese way it is cooked whole. The 12-hour marinating is important.

One 4 to 4½-lb (2 to 2.5 kg) domestic duck

Marinating mixture

4 tbsp. (60 mL) sugar

1 tbsp. (15 mL) salt

4 tbsp. (60 mL) honey

3 tbsp. (50 mL) soy sauce

1/3 cup (80 mL) consommé

****

4 tbsp. (60 mL) cold water

Quarter the duck. Mix together in a large bowl, the sugar, salt, honey, soy sauce and the consommé. Wipe the pieces of duck with lemon juice. Add to the marinating mixture. Mix well to coat the duck with the sauce. Cover and marinate 12 hours in the refrigerator.

To roast the duck, remove from the marinade, and put the pieces in a baking dish. Add the cold water. Do not cover. Preheat the convection oven to 350°F (180°C), 15 minutes. Place the spatter shield in the ceramic tray. Place the rack on top and put the baking dish on it. Cook 35 minutes to 1 hour, turning the pieces of duck halfway through the cooking.

To make the gravy: Add a few spoonfuls of port wine and cream to the drippings in the baking dish. Remove the fat on top and heat the gravy 1 minute at HIGH in the Microwave. Serve.

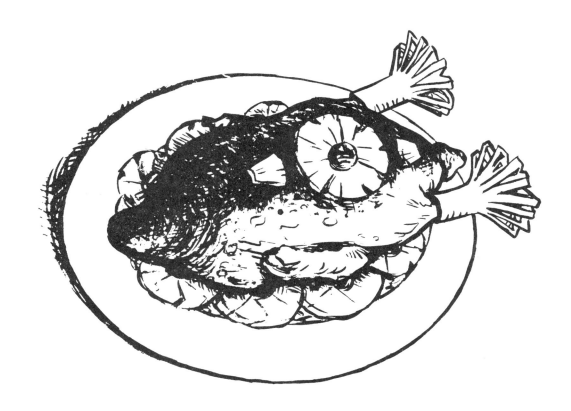

Cantonese Roasted Duck

A browning dish is a must to succeed with this Chinese way to roast duck. Serve with rice or small dumplings.

A 3 to 4-lb (1.5 to 2 kg) domestic duck
2 garlic cloves, chopped fine
1/2 cup (125 mL) chopped green onions
2 tbsp. (30 mL) dry sherry
2 tbsp. (30 mL) soy sauce
1 tsp. (5 mL) ground cardamon
2 tbsp. (30 mL) fresh ginger, thinly sliced
1 tsp. (5 mL) brown sugar
1 tsp. (5 mL) vegetable oil

Basting Sauce:
1 tbsp. (15 mL) honey
1 tbsp. (15 mL) water
1 tsp. (5 mL) rice vinegar*

Place in a glass measuring cup the basting sauce ingredients. Cook 1 minute at HIGH. Stir well. Wash duck under cold running water, wipe inside and out with paper towels. Place on a dry paper towel. Let stand 2 hours, without covering, for the skin to dry.
Combine in a small bowl, the garlic, onion, sherry, soy sauce, cardamon, ginger and brown sugar. Preheat browning dish 7 minutes at HIGH. Do not remove dish from oven. Add the vegetable oil and cook 40 seconds at HIGH. Add the garlic-onion mixture to the hot oil and stir for at least 30 to 40 seconds and pour sauce into the duck. Sew opening so most of the sauce will remain in the duck. Wipe the browning dish and preheat again for 7 minutes. Place the duck in the browning dish, breast-side down.
Brush all over with basting sauce. Cook 10 minutes at HIGH. Turn. Remove drippings from dish and place duck breast-side up on a Microwave rack or an inverted plate placed in the dish. Baste again and repeat cooking at MEDIUM for 15 minutes more. Let duck stand covered for 10 minutes before serving.
Add 1 tablespoon (15 mL) cornstarch to the gravy in the dish, stir well, add 2 tablespoons (30 mL) water. Mix well and cook 2 minutes at HIGH. Stir well. Serve with duck.

* *Japanese rice vinegar is readily available in Oriental food shops. It is mild, slightly sweet and pungent. It may be replaced with cider vinegar.*

Duck Hymettus

A walnut stuffing gives this duck an interesting flavor. I like to serve it with a big bowl of fresh crisp watercress which complements the walnut-bread stuffing. Pour the gravy over the stuffing when serving.

1 domestic duck

The stuffing:

1 tbsp. (15 mL) butter

1/2 cup (125 mL) onion, chopped fine

3/4 cup (190 mL) chopped walnuts

Grated rind of 1 lemon

1 cup (250 mL) diced fresh bread

3 tbsp. (50 mL) chopped parsley

1 tsp. (5 mL) sage

1/2 tsp. (2 mL) thyme

1/2 tsp. (2 mL) cinnamon or allspice

1/2 tsp. (2 mL) ground cardamon (if available)

Salt and pepper to taste

1 egg, lightly beaten

****

2 tbsp. (30 mL) butter

4 tbsp. (60 mL) honey

****

Juice of 1 lemon or 1/4 cup (60 mL) brandy, rum or orange liqueur

****

The gravy:

1 tbsp. (15 mL) flour

3/4 cup (190 mL) chicken consommé

To prepare the stuffing, melt the butter in a bowl, 1 minute at HIGH, add the onion and cook 2 minutes at HIGH. Stir well, add the walnuts, mix and cook 3 minutes at HIGH. Add the remaining stuffing ingredients. Taste for seasoning. Mix well and stuff into the duck. Sew opening with heavy thread, tie legs with a string, then rub breast and legs of duck with the butter and honey creamed together.

Place duck on rack, set in a 12 x 12-inch (30 x 30 cm) ceramic (Corning) dish or other Microwave-safe dish large enough to hold rack and duck.

Sprinkle breast of duck with paprika. Microwave at HIGH 15 minutes. Add lemon juice or brandy or orange liqueur. Cook at MEDIUM 15 to 25 minutes, or until breast meat is soft and leg bones can be moved slightly when twisted.

Place duck on a warm platter and cover with foil. Let stand 15 minutes.

To make the gravy: Add the flour to the drippings. Stir well and add the chicken consommé. Stir and cook 4 to 6 minutes at HIGH. Stir well, cook a minute or two more if necessary, as the gravy should be smooth and light. Stir well.

Ballottine of Duck *(photo page 80-81)*

Without experience it is somewhat difficult to bone a duck. Ask your butcher, or cut through the middle of the back, fold down with your two hands, and start by removing the inside bones, which are very flexible, cutting through here and there. This procedure can be done quickly.

A 4 to 5-lb (2 to 2.5 kg) duck, deboned

Stuffing

2 tbsp. (30 mL) butter

1 onion, peeled and chopped fine

3/4 lb (375 g) ground pork

3/4 cup (190 mL) white breadcrumbs

1 tsp. (5 mL) sage

6 to 8 sprigs parsley, minced

3 tbsp. (50 mL) dry sherry

1 egg, beaten

2 thin slices cooked ham, julienned

2 tbsp. (30 mL) coarsely chopped walnuts

Salt

Freshly ground pepper

Sauce:

1/2 cup (125 mL) chicken broth, homemade or canned condensed

1/2 carrot, thinly sliced

1/2 small onion, peeled and sliced

1 tsp. (5 mL) cornstarch

1/4 cup (60 mL) Madeira

1/3 lb (160 g) mushrooms, sliced

Salt

Freshly ground pepper

To make the stuffing: Combine butter and onion in a glass bowl. Heat 1 minute at HIGH. Combine with ground meat, breadcrumbs, parsley, sage and sherry. Mix in the beaten egg, adding salt and pepper to taste.

Stuff the duck, alternating ham and walnuts (this makes an interesting design when the duck is served), along with the stuffing. Shape the ballottine in a cylinder, as long and as narrow as possible. Sew up with a trussing needle and heavy white thread, threading and tying at regular intervals to keep the ballottine in shape.

Place in a long, narrow glass or earthenware dish. Cook 14 to 18 minutes at MEDIUM-HIGH, and 10 minutes at LOW. Refrigerate when cooled. Slice when cold. If you wish to serve it hot, reheat covered with a lid or waxed paper* 5 minutes at MEDIUM.

If you have a probe: Once you have placed the ballottine in the dish, you insert the probe and set for 160°F (68°C). The oven does the work. When it stops, the duck is cooked. (Consult your oven manual).

To make the sauce: Combine the broth, carrot and onion and cook 5 minutes at MEDIUM-HIGH, stirring once. Strain, pressing with a rubber spatula to extract all the juices. Mix the cornstarch and Madeira and stir until smooth, add to the sauce, stir, add the mushrooms and cook 2 minutes at HIGH, stir. If sufficiently creamy it is ready, if not cook another minute at HIGH.

The sauce can be poured over the sliced duck before it is refrigerated covered, which will form a glaze. To serve hot, pour the hot sauce over the sliced or unsliced ballottine.

* *If you have Micro-Dur dishes use the cover instead of waxed or plastic paper.*

Quail, Partridge and Pheasant

Aberdeen Quail

Scots are very fond of wild birds, so they are masters at cooking them. We have farm-bred quail, but they nonetheless retain a certain "wild flavor". Roasted in the Microwave the Aberdeen way they are super!

3 to 4 quail

Stuffing:

1 cup (250 g) wholewheat bread, diced

1 or 2 wild mushrooms, chopped fine

1/2 cup (125 mL) hot light cream

2 tbsp. (30 mL) whisky of your choice

1 tsp. (5 mL) tarragon or rosemary

1/2 tsp. (2 mL) salt

1/4 tsp. (1 mL) pepper

Coating:

1 tsp. (5 mL) dark brown sugar

1 tsp. (5 mL) Kitchen Bouquet

1/2 tsp. (2 mL) paprika

1 tsp. (5 mL) dry mustard

1 tbsp. (15 mL) soft butter

Wash quail under running water. Drain well. Wipe inside and out with paper towelling.

Prepare stuffing: Place all the ingredients in a bowl. Mash and stir together until thick. Divide into 3 or 4 portions. Stuff each quail with a portion. Tie the bird with a string, fold the wings under.

Coating: Mix the coating ingredients together. Rub all over the quail, with your hands. Preheat a browning dish 7 minutes at HIGH. Without removing the dish from the oven, place each quail on the dish, breast-side down. Cook 5 minutes at HIGH. Turn breast on second side. Cook 5 minutes at HIGH. Place birds on their backs, cook 10 minutes at MEDIUM-HIGH. Test for doneness as sometimes 5 or 6 more minutes are needed, depending on size of the quail.

Remove to a hot platter. To the residue in the dish, add the quail livers, chopped fine, and 3 tablespoons (50 mL) white wine or whisky. Scrape dish. Add 1 teaspoon (5 mL) instant flour. Stir well. Cook 2 to 3 minutes at HIGH, stirring once. Remove from oven. Stir well. Serve with the quail.

Quail Comice

In the South of France, when the season for ripe pears is at its peak, they prepare these delicious quail with fresh pears and pear liqueur. Traditionally, they are served with two elegant vegetables and hot crusty French bread.

6 medium-sized quail	**3 tbsp. (50 mL) brandy or white wine**
6 small garlic cloves	**1 cup (250 mL) peeled and thinly sliced pears**
4 slices of bacon, diced	**1 tbsp. (15 mL) flour**
2 tbsp. (30 mL) soy sauce*	**3 tbsp. (50 mL) cream**
1/2 tsp. (2 mL) paprika	**3 tbsp. (50 mL) brandy**
2 tbsp. (30 mL) soft butter	

Wash quail inside and out with a little brandy. Stuff with a clove of garlic and a bit of diced bacon. Mix together the soy sauce and the paprika. Rub all over the quail, then spread the 2 tablespoons (30 mL) of soft butter evenly over each breast.

Place in a baking dish large enough to hold the quail one next to the other. Add the 3 tablespoons (50 mL) of brandy or white wine and the pears in the bottom of the dish. Cook at HIGH 10 minutes. Baste with juice in bottom of dish. Cook at MEDIUM 20 minutes more or until birds are tender. Test breast meat with the point of a knife or move the little leg bones which should be flexible.

Place birds, on warm platter. Cover to keep warm.

Mix together the cream, flour and brandy. Add to the juice and pears left in the dish. Stir until well blended. Cook 2 minutes at HIGH. Stir, when creamy serve as gravy bowl. No salt or pepper is used in this classic recipe.

* When possible use Japanese "Kikkoman" Soy sauce which is milder than the Chinese.

Quail "à la Bruxelloise" *(photo page 88-89)*

Cracked black pepper, fresh or dried thyme and fresh green grapes are combined to give flavor and elegance of taste to these dainty birds.

Marinade

1/2 cup (125 mL) olive or peanut oil

12 black peppercorns, cracked

6 sprigs of thyme or 1 tsp. (5 mL) dried thyme

1/4 cup (60 mL) parsley, coarsely chopped

6 small quail, split in half

1 tsp. (5 mL) salt

1 tsp. (5 mL) thyme

1/3 cup (80 mL) butter

1 cup (250 mL) white wine or white grape juice

30 to 40 fresh green grapes

Mix the marinade ingredients in Pyrex bowl. Roll each quail half in mixture. Cover and refrigerate overnight to marinate. Remove quail from marinade. Pat dry with paper towels. Season with the salt, pepper and thyme.

Melt the butter in a ceramic (Corning) 12-inch (30 cm) square dish, 5 minutes at HIGH. The butter will be golden brown. Place each quail half in the hot butter, breast-side down.

Cook uncovered 15 minutes at HIGH. Turn quail skin-side up, cook at MEDIUM-LOW 20 minutes. Turn quail once more. Cook at HIGH 5 minutes.

Remove quail from dish. Keep warm. To the juice and fat remaining in the pan, add the grape juice or white wine. Cook 5 minutes at HIGH. Add the grapes one by one, left whole or split in half. Stir well in the juice. Cook 3 minutes at HIGH. Stir well and pour over the quail. Serve with tiny cooked pasta of your choice.*

* *I use little star-shaped pasta that I buy at an Italian shop.*

Partridge with Cabbage

This is always a choice dish. When I am ready to serve, I toast 4 to 6 slices of bread on the convection oven rack at 400°F (200°C). I place a whole or half a partridge on each slice of bread and I surround it with cabbage. The bread is delicious. In France, I was served partridge cooked in this manner, but the slice of bread was soaked with cognac before the partridge was placed on it.

4 to 5 partridge

1/2 lb (250 g) fat salt pork

Paprika

Garlic

4 cups (1 L) green cabbage, chopped

4 to 6 large onions, sliced

1 tbsp. (15 mL) coarse salt

1/2 tsp. (2 mL) fresh ground pepper

1 tsp. (5 mL) thyme

1 cup (250 mL) white wine or red burgundy, cider or apple juice

Clean the partridge with the lemon juice. Set aside. Slice the fat salt pork thinly, place in a baking dish, brown one side 10 minutes at HIGH, stirring once, turn. Sprinkle the partridges with paprika, place them over the browned salt pork, stir. Cook 15 minutes at HIGH, turning the partridges once during the cooking. Remove from dish. Add the onions, garlic and cabbage to the drippings. Stir well, cover and cook 15 minutes at HIGH, stirring halfway through the cooking. Bury the partridges in the cabbage, add salt, pepper, thyme and the chosen liquid. Cover and cook at MEDIUM-LOW 40 to 60 minutes. Check doneness of partridges in last 20 minutes of cooking. As for all wild birds, cooking time will vary. Let stand 20 minutes. Place partridges on toasted bread slices. Surround with the cabbage.

Partridge Casserole

If you are not sure how tender the partridge is, this is the perfect recipe to use. The Italian cook them in the same manner, but serve them with a lightly sweetened "Zabaione". Unusual and delicious.

2 partridge rubbed with orange juice

4 slices of bacon, diced

1 cup (250 mL) small white onions

1 cup (250 mL) thinly sliced mushrooms

1/4 cup (60 mL) Madeira wine

1/2 cup (125 mL) chicken consommé

Juice of 1/2 lemon

Rub the cleaned partridges with the orange juice inside and outside. Tie the legs together with a string. Line the baking dish, an 8 x 8-inch (20 x 20 cm) Corning or Pyrex dish, with the diced bacon. Place the partridges on top. Mix the small onions and the sliced mushrooms. Stuff into the partridge cavities. Pour on top the Madeira wine and the consommé. Salt, pepper to taste. Cover with plastic wrap. Cook at HIGH 20 minutes, uncover, baste the partridges with the juice in the dish. Place birds breast-side down and cook another 20 minutes at MEDIUM. Test for doneness after 15 minutes as it may take a few minutes more or a few minutes less depending on the tenderness of the bird.
Add the lemon juice to the gravy. Add the onions and the mushrooms from inside the partridges. Heat at HIGH 2 minutes. Serve with wild rice.
If you wish to serve with the "Zabaione" here is the way to do it.
Beat the yolks of 3 eggs with 2 tablespoons (30 mL) sugar in a 4-cup (1 L) measure, add a full wine glass of Madeira or Marsala wine. Beat again until well mixed. Cook 2 minutes at HIGH, beat with a whisk, cook 1 minute at MEDIUM-HIGH, beat again and cook another minute at MEDIUM-HIGH. If the sauce is not creamy repeat operation once more as the coldness of the eggs can mean a difference of minutes in the cooking. The sauce should be slightly creamy. Serve hot.

Pheasant "à la Normande"
(Convection)

In French cuisine, "à la Normande" always implies apples and very strong cider. This pheasant follows suit. Roasted in the convection section of the Microwave oven it is a real success.

1 pheasant

1 tsp. (5 mL) paprika

2 tsp. (10 mL) butter

6 to 8 apples, peeled and thinly sliced

3 tbsp. (50 mL) melted butter

1/2 cup (125 mL) cream

Salt and pepper, to taste

3 tbsp. (50 mL) brandy

2 egg yolks, beaten

Clean and truss the pheasant with a wet string. Mix together the paprika and the 2 teaspoons (10 mL) butter. Rub the wings and breast of the pheasant with this butter.
Preheat the convection oven to 375°F (190°C) 15 minutes. Line a baking dish with half the apples. Pour the melted butter on top. Set the pheasant on this bed of apples. Salt and pepper to taste and place the remaining apples all around. Place the dish on the roasting rack. Cook at 375°F (190°C) 1 hour or until the pheasant is golden brown on top and the meat is tender. When cooked, put the pheasant on a warm serving dish. Add the cream and brandy to the apples. Mix well, add the beaten egg yolks. Cook at MEDIUM about 3 minutes in the Microwave, stirring halfway through the cooking. You will have a smooth sauce. Salt to taste. Serve in a sauceboat.

Pheasant "Fines-Herbes"

The combination of rosemary, thyme and dry white wine, gives the pheasant a very special flavor which I think of as "elegant".

2 tbsp. (30 mL) butter

6 green onions, chopped fine

1 tsp. (5 mL) thyme

1/2 tsp. (2 mL) rosemary

1/2 tsp. (2 mL) paprika

1/2 tsp. (2 mL) pepper

1/2 cup (125 mL) dry white wine or vermouth

A 2-lb (1 kg) pheasant, quartered

2 tbsp. (10 mL) cornstarch

1 cup (250 mL) sour cream

Put in a measuring cup or bowl, the butter, green onions, thyme, rosemary, paprika, pepper, white wine or vermouth. Heat at HIGH 4 minutes, stirring twice. This is the basting sauce.
Place pheasant pieces, skin-side down, in a 10-inch (25 cm) dish without overlapping. Baste lightly with a bit of the hot sauce. Heat 10 minutes at MEDIUM-HIGH. Turn pheasant over. Baste again with the basting sauce. Cook 7 minutes at HIGH. Check for doneness with a fork, as it varies. If necessary, cook another 10 minutes at MEDIUM. Remove pheasant to a hot platter. Add remaining basting sauce to drippings. Stir in the cornstarch mixed with a tablespoon (15 mL) of cold water. Mix well. Cook at HIGH 2 minutes, stirring after 1 minute of cooking.
Beat in the sour cream, stirring constantly. Place pheasant in sauce. Sprinkle with salt. Cover and heat 1 minute at MEDIUM. Serve.

Rabbit

Rabbit "à la Française" *(last photo)*

The rabbit, lardons, onions, white wine and leeks, all contribute to the delightful enjoyment of this dish.

1 young rabbit, cut up

1 cup (250 mL) white wine or cider

1 medium onion, thinly sliced

2 garlic cloves, minced

1 bay leaf

1/2 tsp. (2 mL) thyme

3 cloves

1/2 cup (125 mL) diced salt pork fat

1 tbsp. (15 mL) butter

1 tsp. (5 mL) Dijon mustard

20 small onions, peeled

1/4 cup (60 mL) browned flour

1 tsp. (5 mL) savory

3 tbsp. (50 mL) parsley, minced

3 small leeks, thinly sliced

Place the pieces of rabbit in a bowl. Add the white wine or cider, onion, garlic, bay leaf, thyme and cloves. Mix together, cover and marinate 6 to 12 hours, refrigerated.

Place the diced salt pork and the butter in a baking dish. Brown at HIGH 8 to 10 minutes, stirring twice during the cooking. Drain the rabbit from the marinade and put it in the baking dish. Stir well. Cover and cook 10 minutes at HIGH. Stir and add the small onions and the mustard, sprinkle with the browned flour, mix well. Strain the marinating liquid and pour over the rabbit. Add the savory, parsley and leeks. Mix together, cover and simmer 40 minutes at MEDIUM. Stir twice. Check doneness of rabbit and if necessary cook 10 minutes more at MEDIUM. Let stand 15 minutes before serving.

Hare or Rabbit Baden-Baden

I tasted this dish in Germany, on a trip to the "Black Forest". I was so intrigued with the diced prunes and the beer that I asked for the recipe. Adapting it to Microwave cooking made it even better.

1/2 lb (250 gr) dried prunes	1 tsp. (5 mL) thyme
Juice of 1 orange	2 tbsp. (30 mL) bacon fat
A rabbit cut into pieces*	6 small onions peeled, left whole
3 tbsp. (50 mL) browned flour	2 bay leaves
1/2 tsp. (2 mL) salt	1 cup (250 mL) light beer of your choice
1/4 tsp. (1 mL) pepper	1 tbsp. (15 mL) brown sugar

Soak the prunes in the orange juice 10 minutes. Place in a bag, the browned flour, salt, pepper and thyme. Add the pieces of rabbit and shake in bag until well coated with the seasoned flour. Put the bacon fat in a 12 x 12-inch (30 x 30 cm) dish and cook at HIGH 4 minutes. The fat must be very hot. Add the floured rabbit pieces one by one to the hot fat. Cook 5 minutes at HIGH on one side, turn, cook 3 minutes at HIGH. Turn each piece of rabbit again. Add the onions, the undrained prunes, bay leaves, salt, pepper; pour the beer all around. Sprinkle the brown sugar over the liquid.
Cover and cook at HIGH 5 minutes. Reduce heat to MEDIUM and cook 20 to 30 minutes or until meat is tender. Test with a fork. Let stand covered 20 minutes.
Sauce can be thickened by adding a tablespoon (15 mL) of flour to the gravy, beating with a whisk. Cook at MEDIUM 3 to 4 minutes or until creamy. Serve in sauceboat.

* To cut rabbit, remove 4 legs, cut each one in two at joint. Cut back into 4 pieces.

Ballottine of Duck
(page 68)

Terrine of Rabbit

A bit of work is involved to make this terrine, but when you wish to have a special pâté for a buffet, I strongly recommend this one which is always a success. A great plus is that it can be made 2 to 3 days ahead and it will keep refrigerated for 8 days. I surround mine with crisp green watercress and serve it with marinated fresh mushrooms and hot French bread.

A 3 to 4-lb (1.5 - 2 kg) rabbit

1/2 lb (250 g) minced pork

1/4 lb (125 g) minced salt pork

1/2 cup (125 mL) milk

1/2 cup (125 mL) breadcrumbs

2 eggs well beaten

1/4 tsp. (1 mL) each of thyme, marjoram,
   savory

1/4 tsp. (1 mL) each nutmeg and cloves

1/4 tsp. (1 mL) pepper

1 tsp. (5 mL) salt

1/2 cup (125 mL) chopped parsley

1 bay leaf

2 tbsp. (30 mL) brandy or port wine

Remove the meat from the rabbit and put through a meat chopper, together with the rabbit liver and kidneys. Add the minced pork, and salt pork; mix together until very well blended.
Heat the milk, 2 minutes at HIGH. Add the breadcrumbs, mix to make a paste, press hard to remove excess milk, if any. Add the bread paste to the meat.
Beat the eggs with thyme, marjoram, savory, nutmeg, cloves, pepper, salt and parsley. Pour into the meat mixture with the bay leaf, the brandy or port. Beat together until thoroughly blended.
Pack into a 9 x 5-inch (22 x 12.5 cm) bread pan, well buttered. To taste, the bottom of pan may be lined with very thin slices of salt pork. Cover top with a buttered paper. Bake at HIGH 10 minutes, then at MEDIUM 25 minutes. Let stand in oven for 20 minutes when cooking time is over. Cover with foil.
Cool and refrigerate 2 to 3 days before unmolding.

Broths and Stuffings

Chicken Stock

When liquid is needed to steam or boil chicken, the canned type can be used, but chicken stock will double the quality and flavor of a sauce or boiled chicken. It freezes well. I like to freeze mine in a 2-cup (500 mL) container for convenience sake, then uncover it and defrost at HIGH for 5 to 7 minutes, whenever I need it. To make about 10 cups (2.5 L) you will need 3 pounds (1.5 kg) of chicken parts such as wings, back, neck and any piece of skin available. You can buy these from your market, if you ask the butcher to set them aside for you.

I have a box in my freezer where I keep all the above-mentioned, as I cook chicken or turkey. I make 3-pound (1.5 kg) bags and set them together in the box. When needed, I place a 3-lb (1.5 kg) package frozen in the dish, add the other ingredients and cook it 20 minutes longer.

3 lb (1.5 kg) bony chicken parts such as back, neck, end of wings, fat*

A veal bone, when available

12 cups (3 L) hot water

1 large yellow onion, unpeeled

4 whole cloves

2 celery stalks with leaves, cut in half

2 carrots, peeled, cut in four

12 crushed peppercorns

A handful of fresh parsley with stems

1 bay leaf

1 tbsp. (15 mL) thyme

1/2 tsp. (2 mL) summer savory

1 tsp. (5 mL) tarragon

Place the ingredients in a 16-cup (4 L) bowl. Cover and cook 30 minutes at HIGH. Let cool in its pot, which may take from 3 to 6 hours. Strain through a fine sieve. Salt to taste, preferably with coarse salt. Keep refrigerated or freeze. Yield: 12 cups (3 L).

* *You may replace the chicken parts with a cooked poultry carcass, the gravy and vegetables added to the broth. Cooking time remains the same. Cool in the cooking dish. Strain and keep in the refrigerator or freezer.*

Giblet Broth

To make a tasty turkey or roasted chicken gravy, if you do not have chicken stock, use the cooked giblet broth as part of the liquid. The slight effort required to make it means the difference between a dull and a tasty gravy.

Giblets and neck from turkey	1/2 tsp. (2 mL) thyme
1 tsp. (5 mL) salt	1 medium onion, cut in four
8 peppercorns	1/2 cup (125 mL) chopped celery or leaves
2 whole cloves	1 small carrot, sliced
1 bay leaf	3 cups (750 mL) boiling water

Remove heart, liver, gizzard and neck from turkey or chicken. Rinse in cold water and rub all over with half a lemon.

Place in an 8-cup (2 L) saucepan, add all the remaining ingredients. Cook at HIGH 10 minutes. Remove the liver and set aside. Cover the dish and cook at HIGH 20 minutes. Let stand one hour, then strain through a fine sieve.

Chop the giblets which are tender, add to the liver, and to the broth, if you wish.

This can be cooked, strained, chopped, etc., then refrigerated covered, overnight.

Flavored Breadcrumbs

This coating replaces commercial mixes. It keeps for several months, refrigerated in a jar or plastic container. This recipe yields 2 cups (500 mL).

2 cups (500 mL) breadcrumbs	1/4 tsp. (1 mL) garlic powder
2 tbsp. (30 mL) peanut oil	1/2 tsp. (2 mL) thyme
2 tsp. (10 mL) pepper	1 tsp. (5 mL) savory
1/2 tsp. (2 mL) salt	1/2 tsp. (2 mL) turmeric
1 tsp. (5 mL) paprika	1/2 tsp. (2 mL) curry powder

Mix all the ingredients together in a bowl. Cook 30 seconds at HIGH. Stir thoroughly. Let stand 10 minutes. Pour into a clean and dry container. Cover and refrigerate.

All-Purpose Bread Stuffing

One of the best stuffing recipes I know. It can be reduced or doubled without changing the flavor and quality. I prefer to cook it in a baking dish, rather than in the bird's cavity, but again you are free to use it as a stuffing or as a casserole.

4 cups (1 L) toasted brown or rye bread

2 cups (500 mL) onions, chopped fine

2 cups (500 mL) diced celery and leaves

1 tsp. (5 mL) thyme

1 tsp. (5 mL) summer savory

1 tsp. (5 mL) salt

1/2 tsp. (2 mL) pepper

1/2 cup (125 mL) melted butter or margarine

1/3 cup (80 mL) sherry, brandy or
    chicken broth

Mix together the toasted bread cut into small dice, the onions, celery, thyme, savory, salt and pepper. Melt the butter or margarine 1 minute at HIGH, add the liquid of your choice. Heat at HIGH 2 minutes.
To stuff the turkey, place half the bread mixture in the turkey, pour half of the hot liquid mixture over the bread. Repeat with the remaining ingredients. Sew the opening with strong thread.
To cook as a casserole: Use the same ingredients. Place half the bread mixture in the bottom of a Microwave-safe loaf pan, pour half the liquid on top, repeat, cover with waxed paper or a lid. Let stand 1 hour at room temperature. Then when ready, cook covered 18 minutes at MEDIUM.
Variations: If you like meat in the stuffing, pass the giblets through the mincer, add 1/2 pound (250 g) minced pork.
Melt 2 tablespoons (30 mL) butter 1 minute at HIGH. Add the meats. Stir well, cover and cook 3 minutes at MEDIUM-HIGH. Add meat to bread mixture. Then proceed same as above — to either stuff the turkey or make a casserole.

Quebec Potato Stuffing

This is one of the most traditional stuffings of Quebec cuisine. It is full of flavor.

The heart, gizzard and liver from the chicken*
1 tbsp. (15 mL) chicken fat or other fat
3 medium onions, finely chopped
1 garlic clove, minced
4 cups cooked potatoes, peeled

2 tsp. (10 mL) savory
1 tbsp. (15 mL) salt
1/2 tsp. (2 mL) pepper
1 tbsp. (15 mL) butter

Put the heart, gizzard and liver through the meat grinder. Melt the chopped fat 5 minutes at HIGH. Stir after 2 minutes. Add the minced giblets, stir. Cook 3 minutes at MEDIUM-HIGH. Add the onions, garlic, savory, salt and pepper. Stir well. Cook 2 minutes at HIGH. Cook the potatoes (see Vegetable Volume). Mash them and mix with the cooked giblets. Add the butter and stir well. Place in a dish, cover with lid or waxed paper. Cook 10 minutes at MEDIUM-HIGH.

* If you prefer, replace the chopped giblets with 1 pound (500 g) minced pork, or use the two meats for a richer stuffing.

English Bread Stuffing

Enough to stuff a 10 to 12-pound (5 to 6 kg) turkey.

1 cup (250 mL) butter or diced turkey fat
1 tbsp. (15 mL) summer savory or sage
1½ tsp. (7 mL) salt
1/4 tsp. (1 mL) pepper

1/2 cup (125 mL) fresh parsley, minced
3/4 cup (190 mL) celery with leaves, chopped
3 cups (750 mL) chopped onions
10 to 11 cups (2.5 - 2.75 L) dry bread, diced

Melt in a large bowl, the butter or diced turkey fat, 2 minutes at HIGH for the butter, 4 minutes at HIGH for the diced fat, stirring once.
Add the summer savory or sage, salt, pepper, parsley, celery and onions. Mix well. Cook 6 minutes at MEDIUM-LOW stirring once.
Pour over the diced bread. Mix well. Taste for seasoning.

Quail "à la Bruxelloise"
(page 73)

Dutch Bread and Potato Stuffing

This can be used with chicken, turkey, duck. When using this stuffing with any kind of bird, wash bird inside and out with Dutch Gin (Geneva Gin).

2 eggs

2 cups (500 mL) milk

4 cups (1 L) coarse breadcrumbs

1/4 tsp. (1 mL) pepper

1 tbsp. (15 mL) salt

2 cups (500 mL) cooked potatoes, mashed

1/2 cup (125 mL) celery, chopped fine

1/4 cup (60 mL) butter

1 large onion, chopped or
    10 green onions, chopped fine

Beat the eggs until light, add the milk and pour over the dry breadcrumbs. Add the salt, pepper, mashed potatoes and celery. Mix together.
Melt the butter, 2 minutes at HIGH, add the onion or green onions, stir until well coated with the butter, cook at HIGH 3 minutes, stirring once.
Pour over the mixture. Mix well and use to stuff turkey, chicken, duck or pheasant.

French Cuisine Turkey Stuffing

One way to flavor the inside of a turkey, which permeates the whole bird as it cooks. Especially recommended for a turkey weighing from 9 to 12 pounds (4.5 to 6 kg). Furthermore, it is quick and easy. This stuffing may also be used with a chicken 5 pounds (2.5 kg) or more or a 4-pound (2 kg) duck.

2 garlic cloves, chopped fine

10 peppercorns, crushed

1 tsp. (5 mL) sage

3 tbsp. (50 mL) margarine

A 6-inch (15 cm) length of French bread

Mix together the garlic, peppercorns, sage and margarine. Spread all over the French bread. Place as is in the turkey cavity, and roast according to the recipe you are following.

Smoked Oyster Stuffing

A Scandinavian way to stuff turkey, featuring smoked oysters coupled with raisins and walnuts. I sometimes use it with quail or pheasant.

1½ cups (375 mL) bread croutons

1 cup (250 mL) milk

1 cup (250 mL) coarsely chopped celery

1 large onion, chopped fine

1/2 cup (125 mL) raisins

1/2 cup (125 mL) chopped walnuts

A 3.62-oz can (104 g) smoked oysters

1/2 cup (125 mL) butter or margarine, melted

Place all the ingredients in a large bowl, toss together until well mixed. Add salt to taste.
Fill cavity loosely as the dressing expands while cooking.
This quantity is sufficient for a 7 to 12-pound (3.5 to 6 kg) turkey.

Goose Apple Stuffing

Cut the recipe in half and use to stuff duck and pheasant. This is one of my favorites. I sometimes add 1/2 cup (125 mL) chopped pears.

2 cups (500 mL) soft breadcrumbs

4 tbsp. (60 mL) butter

1 small onion, chopped fine

1 cup (250 mL) chopped walnuts or pecans

1 tsp. (5 mL) basil or oregano

2 tbsp. (30 mL) milk

2 unpeeled apples, grated

Salt to taste

Use center of loaf (no crust) to make crumbs. Melt butter 2 minutes at HIGH, add the onion and chopped nuts, stir well, cook 2 minutes at HIGH. Add the basil or oregano, milk, bread and apples. Mix well and salt to taste.
Stuff the bird loosely as this stuffing expands.

Apple Raisin Goose Stuffing

If you like apples and raisins in bread stuffing, try this one. For me, there is none better.

1/4 cup (60 mL) soft butter

1 cup (250 mL) chopped onion

1 cup (250 mL) finely diced celery

1 tsp. (5 mL) salt

1/2 tsp. (2 mL) pepper

3 cups (750 mL) diced toasted bread

2 tsp. (10 mL) anise seeds

2 cups (500 mL) unpeeled grated apples

4 tbsp. (60 mL) Madeira or port wine

2/3 cup (160 mL) raisins

Melt the butter in a 4-cup (1 L) bowl 2 minutes at HIGH. Add the onion and celery, stir well. Cook 4 minutes at HIGH, stirring twice. Add all the remaining ingredients. Stir well. Stuff the goose, sew up with thread.

Wild Rice Stuffing

Use with duck or quail — double for roasted chicken.

The bird liver or
   1/2 lb (250 g) chicken liver

3 tbsp. (50 mL) butter

6 green onions, chopped

4 tbsp. (60 mL) chicken consommé

1 cup (250 mL) wild rice

1/4 tsp. (1 mL) curry powder

Chop the liver into small pieces with a sharp knife. Melt the butter in a dish 5 minutes at HIGH, it will brown. Add green onions, stir well. Add the chicken consommé. Cook 3 minutes at HIGH. Salt, pepper to taste. Set aside.
Bring 4 cups (1 L) of water to boil, 12 minutes at HIGH. Add the wild rice and curry. Stir well. Cover and cook 30 minutes at MEDIUM. Let stand 10 minutes.
When rice is ready, add the green onion mixture. Mix well. Taste for salt and use.

Sauces

Giblet Gravy

Gravy for all roasted birds, especially turkey and chicken, can be made according to this recipe.

1/2 cup (125 mL) fat from roasted fowl drippings

1/3 cup (80 mL) all-purpose or instant flour

1 garlic clove, crushed or chopped fine

3 cups (375 mL) strained giblet broth*

1/4 cup (60 mL) sherry or Madeira or red wine

When roasted, set bird on a warm plate. Pour drippings into a bowl. Let the fat rise to the top, this should take 3 to 4 minutes. Skim off 1/2 cup (125 mL) of the fat on top, add the flour, stir until well mixed, add the garlic, and giblet broth.

Remove all fat left in drippings. Add remaining juice to flour mixture. Heat at HIGH 6 to 8 minutes, stirring twice. It will give a light creamy gravy. Taste for salt.

Variations: To your choice add either of the following.
- 1 cup (250 mL) thinly sliced mushrooms to the gravy, before the last 4 minutes of cooking;
- 1 cup (250 mL) thinly sliced onions. Cook same as above;
- 1 cup (250 mL) canned unsweetened chestnuts chopped coarsely;
- 1/2 cup (125 mL) cranberry sauce or diced orange.

* See Giblet Broth recipe.

Basting Sauce for Duck

Simply place cleaned duck, split in half or legs tied, in a ceramic (Corning) dish and cook by Microwave or by convection. I sometimes use this sauce over chicken breasts.

1/2 cup (125 mL) fresh orange juice

1/2 cup (125 mL) chili sauce

1/4 cup (60 mL) each honey and Worcestershire sauce

3 garlic cloves, chopped fine

A small onion, chopped fine

1/4 tsp. (1 mL) pepper

Mix all the ingredients together. Brush generously inside and outside the bird (chicken, quail or duck). Follow instructions given for cooking chosen bird by convection or Microwave.
Each type of bird, duck, quail, chicken, pheasant, etc. will have a different flavor, although the same basting sauce is used.

Orange Sauce for Duck

I serve this sauce with duck but also use it often to warm up thinly sliced leftover duck.

1 cup (250 mL) fresh orange juice

1 tbsp. (15 mL) cornstarch

3 tbsp. (50 mL) sugar

2 tbsp. (30 mL) Grand Marnier or other orange liqueur

Grated rind of 1/2 an orange

Mix the cornstarch with the orange juice. Add the sugar, stir well. Cook at MEDIUM-HIGH 4 minutes, stirring after 3 minutes; add the orange rind and the liqueur. Stir well. Heat 1 minute at HIGH. Serve.

Simple Port Wine Sauce

Simple but delicious with all types of birds, especially pheasant.

1/2 cup (125 mL) port wine
2 large green onions, chopped fine
Juice of 1/2 a lemon

Mix the ingredients in a bowl. Microwave at HIGH 2 minutes. Add to any bird gravy or pour over leftover meat, thinly sliced. Cover with waxed paper and cook 1 to 2 minutes at MEDIUM-HIGH, time depends on quantity.

Port Wine Sauce for Duck

Use this to reheat leftovers or to serve as an extra sauce with your favorite duck recipe.

1/2 cup (125 mL) port wine   **Salt, pepper to taste**
4 green onions chopped   **2 tsp. (10 mL) cornstarch**
1/4 tsp. (1 mL) thyme   **Grated rind of 1 orange**
1/2 cup (125 mL) fresh orange juice **1 orange cut into sections**
1 cup (250 mL) chicken consommé

Place in a bowl, the port wine, green onions, thyme and orange juice. Stir until well mixed. Boil at HIGH about 20 minutes or until reduced to half. Stir 2 to 3 times during the cooking period. Add 1/2 cup (125 mL) of chicken consommé. Boil 3 minutes at HIGH. Salt, pepper to taste. Mix together the cornstarch, the remaining chicken consommé, orange rind and sections. Add to wine mixture and stir. Cook 3 to 4 minutes at HIGH, stirring once. The sauce should be light and creamy.

Glaze for Roasted Birds

A glaze brushed on chicken, large or small, before cooking, gives it a shiny coating and a delicious flavor. It is well to brush the under part of the chicken when it is turned over as some recipes call for. If you have never used a glaze, try the one of your choice on chicken legs or wings. Since these parts are less expensive than chicken breasts, you will learn how to do it and see the result.

Duck, quail, turkey, etc. can be glazed as well as chicken. Whenever I use one of the following glazes during the cooking, I like to brush it all over the bird when it is cooked, just before serving. I usually add a tablespoon (15 mL) of brandy, scotch, rye or rum to the last touch of glaze.

French Glaze for Turkey and Large Chicken

1/2 cup (125 mL) butter	2 tsp. (10 mL) thyme
2 tsp. (10 mL) savory	1 tsp. (5 mL) Kitchen Bouquet
2 tsp. (10 mL) tarragon	1 tbsp. (15 mL) chicken Bovril

Place all the ingredients in a bowl. Cook 2 minutes at HIGH. Stir well. Brush on turkey or large roasting chicken just before putting it into the Microwave. Roast as directed by the recipe. Baste once halfway through the roasting period and once when bird is ready.

Plum Glaze for Duck, Quail and Pheasant

1 can purple plum	2 tbsp. (30 mL) lemon juice
3 tbsp. (50 mL) corn syrup	Rind of 1 orange

Wash and drain all the plums, add all the other ingredients. Cook at HIGH for 2 minutes. Stir well. Use this sauce like the French glaze, before, during and after roasting the bird of your choice.

Oriental Glaze

This can be used with all types of birds, chickens, etc. except turkey.

2 tsp. (10 mL) cornstarch

1/4 cup (60 mL) soy sauce

1 tbsp. (15 mL) sesame oil

2/3 cup (160 mL) water

Combine the cornstarch and soy sauce in a bowl. Stir in the sesame oil and the water. Cook at HIGH 2 minutes, stirring twice.

Use this sauce as the French glaze, before, during and after roasting the bird of your choice.

Port Wine Jelly

To me, this is a must with roast goose. It can be made in advance, as it will keep 10 to 15 days refrigerated. The best port wine to use is a Portuguese type, but if you do not have it use a good quality Canadian port.

1/2 cup (125 mL) sugar

1 cup (250 mL) water

The grated peel and juice of 1 lemon

1 envelope unflavored gelatine

1 cup (250 mL) port wine

Place in a large measuring cup, the sugar, water and grated lemon rind. Cook at HIGH 4 minutes. Stir well.

Meanwhile soak the gelatine in the lemon juice.

Add the soaked gelatine to the hot mixture. Stir well. Cook 1 minute at MEDIUM-HIGH. Let cool 10 minutes, then add the port wine. Stir well. Pour into an attractive serving dish. Cover and refrigerate until set.

English Tart Applesauce

I was given this most interesting sauce in Lambourn, England, by a race horse trainer. It is a perfect cold fruit sauce to serve with goose.

6 to 8 apples	**1 cup (250 mL) milk**
2 tbsp. (30 mL) butter	**1 tsp. (5 mL) cider or wine vinegar**
1/2 tsp. (2 mL) curry powder	**2 tbsp. (30 mL) chopped fresh mint**
2 tbsp. (30 mL) flour	

Peel, core and slice the apples. Melt the butter 1 minute at HIGH. Add the curry powder and stir until well blended. Stir in the flour and add the milk. Stir well. Cook at MEDIUM-HIGH 3 to 4 minutes, or until creamy and smooth, stirring twice during the cooking period.
Add the apples, mix well, cover and cook at MEDIUM-LOW about 10 to 15 minutes, stirring twice. Then beat until the apples are reduced to a pulp. Taste for seasoning and add the cider or wine vinegar and the chopped mint. Serve hot.
This sauce can be made 4 to 5 days in advance and kept refrigerated. When ready to serve, reheat 2 to 4 minutes at MEDIUM-HIGH. Stir well and serve.

Mayonnaise "chaud-froid"

A "chaud-froid" is used to coat cold slices of cooked chicken or any other type of bird. An elegant way to serve it cold in the summer or to serve cold leftovers at any time.

1 tbsp. (15 mL) unflavored gelatine
2 tbsp. (30 mL) cold water or white wine
2 cups (500 mL) mayonnaise of your choice

Measure the cold water in a cup, add the gelatine, let stand 1 minute. Cook at MEDIUM 1 to 2 minutes or until mixture is like clear water. Pour slowly into the cold mayonnaise, stirring vigorously with a whisk. Place slices of cooked chicken on a piece of waxed paper, and coat with the mayonnaise, spreading it with a spatula. Lift meat and place in dish. When all is done, refrigerate to set about 30 minutes. Surround chicken with watercress or crisp lettuce leaves or parsley. In the summer when I have fresh tarragon leaves or dill, I add about a tablespoon (15 mL) of either herb, when adding the gelatine.

General Index

Give the **Encyclopedia of Microwave Cooking** to a friend!

Éditions Héritage
300, Arran, Saint-Lambert, Quebec
J4R 1K5

Send to:

NAME: _____

STREET: _____

PROVINCE: _____ *POSTAL CODE:* _____

____ copy(ies) of: **Meats and Sauces $14.95**

____ copy(ies) of: **Soups and Garnishes $14.95**

____ copy(ies) of: **Fish and Sauces $14.95**

____ copy(ies) of: **Poultry, Stuffing and Sauces $14.95**

____ copy(ies) of: **Vegetables and their Sauces $14.95**

Enclosed is $ per book plus $1.00 each for postage and handling. Total amount enclosed:
$_____
Make cheque or money order payable to Éditions Héritage. Prices subject to change without notice.

- ✂

Give the **Encyclopedia of Microwave Cooking** to a friend!

Éditions Héritage
300, Arran, Saint-Lambert, Quebec
J4R 1K5

Send to:

NAME: _____

STREET: _____

PROVINCE: _____ *POSTAL CODE:* _____

____ copy(ies) of: **Meats and Sauces $14.95**

____ copy(ies) of: **Soups and Garnishes $14.95**

____ copy(ies) of: **Fish and Sauces $14.95**

____ copy(ies) of: **Poultry, Stuffing and Sauces $14.95**

____ copy(ies) of: **Vegetables and their Sauces $14.95**

Enclosed is $ per book plus $1.00 each for postage and handling. Total amount enclosed:
$_____
Make cheque or money order payable to Éditions Héritage. Prices subject to change without notice.

Printed by
PAYETTE & SIMMS, INC.
in February, 1986
at Saint-Lambert, Qué.